WESSEX

Travels and Short Breaks

Sally Lunn's House, Bath

WESSEX

Travels and Short Breaks

DAVID HEWSON

Illustrations by Ray Evans

MEREHURST
LONDON

Published 1990 by Merehurst Limited
Ferry House, 51-57 Lacy Road
Putney, London SW15 1PR
Copyright ©David Hewson 1990
ISBN 1 85391 088 0

Designed and produced by Snap! Books
Typeset by TRS Graphics
Illustrations by Ray Evans
Maps by Chris Shaw
Cover photograph: Kimmeridge Bay and village,
Dorset, by courtesy of ZEFA Picture Library (UK) Ltd

Printed in Great Britain by Butler and Tanner,
Frome, Somerset
Colour separations by Oxted Colour Printers
Ltd, Surrey

Contents

Old Sarum, Wiltshire

Author's Preface

The very name of Wessex conjures up many agreeable images in the mind of the traveller in Britain: the lively bucolic communities of Thomas Hardy, old, deeper legends of King Arthur and the elusive Holy Grail, and the lost Saxon kingdom of Alfred. Yet few of us could, with any certainty, draw the boundaries of this tempting domain on any modern map of the nation. Wessex is a state of mind, a mental picture of pre-industrial Britain, more than an exact geographical definition.

The aim of this book is to offer a practical, personal introduction to this ill-defined region of ancient history, curious delights and unusual beauty. Like the other books in this series, this is not an attempt to produce a comprehensive gazeteer to this large and varied part of Britain. The areas of interest mentioned here are, in the author's opinion, those which offer the greatest reward to the modern traveller who, almost invariably, has a fixed period of time in which to discover the area and few spare hours to spend on minor sights. Definitive, scholarly guidebooks have their place in the scheme of things, but this is not one of them. I have tried to set down for the reader some easy and convenient ways by which he or she will begin to appreciate some of the finer points of Wessex. There are several delightful areas for weekend breaks within the region, but, as with all brief holidays, it is vital to know what is worth seeing and what is not, and to have an idea of the best places to stay and eat.

For the purpose of this book I have divided Wessex into six separate regions. For each I describe the principal sights and close each section with a listing of worthwhile hotels, restaurants, stately homes, countryside walks, museums and other diversions. There is no reason why some, or indeed all, of these six separate elements cannot be joined together to make a longer holiday. It must be said that these divisions are wholly of my own making and are designed more for the convenience of the traveller than to preserve historical accuracy or the lines of modern local government boundaries. Those who know the area will doubtless protest of omissions; these are inevitable in a book of this nature, but visiting the six parts outlined here will provide the traveller with a sound introduction to this most pleasant part of Britain and the basis for return trips which can accomplish more in the way of detailed observation. Two omissions should be explained. I have shied away from the Avon coastline and the rather drab resort of Weston-super-Mare because the area has little regional character or relevance to the subject matter of this book. Winchester, though a delightful city and the historic capital of Alfred's Wessex, poses geographical difficulties. Its location north east of Southampton on the motorway to London rather detaches the place from the countryside which it once ruled; a worthwhile detour but one which is somewhat out of keeping with the spirit of journeys to the west.

From Stonehenge to Swanage, Wessex has much to offer the traveller. It is less brash in its pursuit of the tourist than the neighbouring West Country and, thanks to the modern motorway network, infinitely more accessible. The countryside is varied and unpredictable, from the flat Somerset Levels, rich in wildlife, to the dramatic and wild coastline of Dorset. Some of the most engaging villages and towns in Britain can be found here – the unique home of modern mystics in Glastonbury, picturesque Lyme Regis, handsome Shaftesbury and the Georgian splendours of Blandford Forum. The cities are famous throughout the world, Bristol, Bath, Exeter, Taunton and Salisbury, each with its unique identity. The visitor will soon choose a favourite: Bath, with its Roman and Georgian wonders, Salisbury's famous cathedral and Close, or Bristol's maritime, cosmopolitan character. All are worth visiting.

The proximity of Wessex to London has had a happy effect on the area's facilities for travellers. Good hotels and restaurants have been in demand here for decades, catering for all tastes and pockets. One can spend a small fortune in the luxury of Taunton's Castle Hotel or travel more cheaply, in excellent small hotels, eating in more modest locally run establishments. Nowhere in Britain has a poorer excuse for serving disappointing food and drink; fish, crab, meat and vegetables are available locally, cider and beer are deservedly famous and several acclaimed English vineyards are active in the region.

The attractions of Wessex are visual, cultural and personal. This is a part of the country where the traveller may walk in gorgeous countryside in the morning, visit an ancient cathedral in the afternoon and sit down to an excellent meal in a speciality fish restaurant a few yards from the English Channel in the evening. Small wonder that the area has more than its fair share of devotees, as much in love as Thomas Hardy ever was with his mythical countryside based on Dorset.

This book was researched independently of all tourist interests in the area, since it seems plain to me that the only fair guidebooks are those written from the viewpoint of the reader. It is easy to win welcoming smiles from hotels and restaurants when they are aware that a mention in a book is in the offing, but this says nothing for the sort of greeting the ordinary, footsore traveller will receive from the same establishment. I have listed the principal tourist information centres in the areas visited and recommend them as sources of impartial advice and local detail. The accommodation services are frequently excellent and can turn up happy surprises at remarkably low prices. While every effort has been made to ensure that the opening times of the organisations listed are accurate, do bear in mind that these details change. They can always be confirmed through the local tourist information centres where advance planning is required.

St Ann Gate, Salisbury

9

Corfe Castle, Dorset

The Faces of Wessex

No-one can state with any degree of certainty the precise boundaries of Wessex. Thomas Hardy's own borders for the fictional country he created encompass the Isle of Wight, Oxford and parts of Cornwall; the historic limits of the Saxon kingdom called Wessex were at best shifting and at worst almost completely undefined. Modern Wessex may be thought of as comprising parts of the counties of Avon, Wiltshire, Dorset, Somerset and Devon. One may argue about where the exact borderline falls, but the limits of the region – the Severn to the north, Cornwall to the west, the Test or Avon to the east and the Channel to the south – seem self evident.

This is a curiously polyglot part of Britain, happily lacking the uniform character by which one can label 'the north', 'the south' or 'the West Country'. It has, in Bristol and, to a lesser extent the larger towns and cities of the south of the region, a considerable industrial base, but not one which spills over into the neighbouring countryside communities. The area is sufficiently distant from London and the south east to have escaped, for the most part, the fate of suburbia, but sadly it is beginning to suffer from partial colonisation by second home owners. However, thousands still flock to the West Country without stopping for a moment in the lovely counties of the 'mid-West'; there are very few examples of the whitewashed, expatriate holiday village which one finds everywhere in Cornwall (the best example being Polperro).

10

Wessex, while not unmindful of the tourist trade, has somehow managed to absorb the visitors it requires without turning itself into a side show. In the more popular areas the visitor will find several of the nicest seaside resorts in Britain, such as Swanage, Poole, Lyme Regis and Budleigh Salterton. Out in the countryside the villages are, in the main, unspoilt, well-preserved and thoroughly charming. This is no accident. Those communities which have escaped the worst of the planning disasters of the last three decades have been the ones which have set their faces against wholesale redevelopment. And Wessex houses an argumentative people when roused. No planning application escapes scrutiny, no 'refurbishment' avoids a thorough examination by those affected. There are disappointments, of course, and Hardy's beloved Dorchester is one of them. But, by and large, one is hard pressed to find any part of Britain which has so resolutely resisted the demolition man.

History

The great prehistoric monuments of Stonehenge and Avebury bear witness to the presence of early man in south west Britain. But these are only the two best known relics of prehistoric man; many others await the visitor, from Cadbury Castle, reputed to be the site of the mythical Camelot, to Old Sarum, the original location of Salisbury. Traces of human occupation have been found which can be dated back to the earliest days of man, some half a million years ago, when England was still part of the continental land mass. There is evidence that there was a substantial population in the area before the geological changes which made England an island around 6500 BC. Stonehenge and Avebury began to appear around 2800 BC and were gradually changed and developed over the next millennium. Two thousand years separate the first phase of Stonehenge from Iron Age man who created the hillforts which still dot the region, South Cadbury, Maiden Castle and Danebury among them.

The Romans invaded Britain in AD 43 and faced an island divided into individual tribal kingdoms with little chance of resisting the well-trained forces of Rome. Bath – Aquae Sulis – provides us with the best known Roman remains in Britain, the hot spring baths which were a social focus of British life under Roman occupation. There were also important settlements at Winchester, Salisbury and Dorchester. The

11

Romans brought new skills to English life, farming, fiscal organisation, road construction and other public works. For 400 years, the region prospered on trade with other parts of the empire. Then, with the collapse of Rome, the Dark Ages began, an era of which we still know little. The central organisation of the Roman state collapsed as forces from northern Europe fought to take over the land. The Wessex heroes of Arthur and Alfred date from this bleak period, icons of national identity in whom myth and reality blend seamlessly.

The nation of Wessex appeared in the sixth century, stretching at one time as far as Berkshire. Alfred, who ruled from Winchester, held his fragile kingdom together with a famous victory against the encroaching Vikings in AD 878 which paved the way for a briefly united England under his successors. The wealth of lovely church architecture found in the region today – the cathedrals of Wells and Salisbury are among the best examples – is largely a legacy of the Normans who followed.

Medieval Wessex prospered on trade, wool and agriculture. Great country estates appeared, often owned by important men of state. Walter Raleigh lived, for a time, at Sherborne Castle, a gift from Elizabeth I who was later to imprison him. The Civil War divided the region much as it did the rest of Britain. The most spectacular siege in the area was that of Corfe Castle, twice defended heroically by Lady Banks until she was betrayed into surrender.

The region suffered another bloody conflict only 40 years after the Civil War when it was the scene of the Monmouth or 'Pitchfork' rebellion. Charles II, who was restored to the throne in 1660, was succeeded by his Catholic brother, James II. Charles's illegitimate son, the Duke of Monmouth, landed at Lyme Regis in 1685 with three ships and 80 men, claiming the throne for himself and promising to return the monarchy to Protestant ways. The rebels attracted much local support and in Taunton Monmouth was declared king. The rebel cause prospered briefly and at one time seemed poised to threaten Bristol.

On July 5 Monmouth's forces left Bridgwater and attempted to cross Sedgemoor with the royal army only half a mile away. The royal camp was awoken by a mysterious shot and a bloody battle fought in the dark. Monmouth was captured and beheaded in London. In the Castle at Taunton and elsewhere Judge Jeffreys set up his 'Bloody Assizes' to try those who had fought for the rebel army. In all, he sentenced more than 300 to be publicly hanged, drawn and quartered and a further 600 were transported for life, mostly to work as slaves in the West Indies. The vengeance taken by Jeffreys provoked bitter memories in Wessex for many years thereafter. James II still proved insecure; three years after the rebellion he was deposed and his Protestant daughter ruled in his place with her husband William of Orange. The route of the Pitchfork Rebellion is now marked as a trail of 115 miles running from Lyme Regis to Bridgwater, then in a circle to Glastonbury, Pensford, Keynsham, Bath, Frome and Shepton Mallet back to Bridgwater.

In Regency times, Bath took on a new significance as one of the first fashionable resorts. The presence of characters like Beau Nash, and a supporting cast of artists, society ladies and gentlemen and the occasional rogue, briefly turned Bath into a focal point of British society.

During the Victorian era the growth of the railways brought trade and prosperity to the principal coastal towns and cities. Bristol, always an important port, took on a new significance for the growing Victorian empire. At the same time, the train introduced a new form of cheap, fast travel for the Victorian public and encouraged the growth of seaside resorts. This was also the era of unrest on the land. Six farm labourers in Dorset became world famous when they were prosecuted and transported for forming an illegal trade union. The Tolpuddle Martyrs are remembered today as pioneers of the modern trade unions.

Modern Wessex embraces traditional agriculture, up-to-the-minute shipping ports, sleepy, prosperous country towns and hectic industrial parks. Better transport links threaten to bring the region further into the realm of the prosperous south east – already Bath and Bristol are proving popular places to live for London commuters making use of the fast train services into the capital. But the essential character of the region remains unique and independent, and long shall it remain so.

Geography and Wildlife

The landscape of Wessex is as varied as any in Britain, ranging from the wild Dorset coastline to the majestic Marlborough Downs. Perhaps the most spectacular sight is the Cheddar Gorge, a dramatic gash in the limestone landscape of the Mendips which attracts many thousands of visitors each year. But more inaccessible beauty spots remain quiet even at the height of summer.

Few areas can match Wessex's lovely tracts of open land. Salisbury Plain, though used, in part, for military manoeuvres, stretches north from Salisbury to Devizes, crossed by the rivers Avon and Wylye, the scene of excellent open countryside walks and several ancient monuments dating back to prehistoric times. The hills of Cranborne Chase were used as a royal hunting preserve for centuries and still offer secluded views of the neighbouring area. The Isle of Purbeck and the lesser known Somerset Levels also provide attractive and interesting walking country. There are countryside parks at Durlston, near Swanage, Upton Park, near Poole, and Barton Farm, near Bradford-upon-Avon, and innumerable private countryside facilities throughout the region, from exquisite cottage gardens to the commercialism of Longleat with its safari park.

The backbone of Wessex life for centuries has been agriculture, often carried out as part of the management of a great estate. Estate owners have included the great families of England, the Crown, the Church, famous university colleges and the Duchy of Cornwall, between them concentrating ownership of the land into a limited number of hands, creating magnificent country houses and castles and large estate grounds for use as deer parks. It is the dominance of land ownership by a few which explains the existence of large tracts of open land in the region today, and the proliferation of country mansions like Ston Easton and Dyrham Park, construction tasks which attracted the great names of landscape gardening in the 18th century, such as Capability Brown and Humphrey Repton. At the same time, the villages developed almost along feudal lines, with tied cottages for agricultural labour, producing an economically dependent, impoverished society recorded by Hardy and opposed by those early Dorset trade unionists, the Tolpuddle Martyrs.

Modern Wessex farming is hardly untouched by the 20th century, but the growth of the corporate farm, which has spelled the end of the small mixed estate in some parts of the country, is less here than it might have been. In the small towns of the region the sharp-eyed visitor can still spot the 'farming folk' out on their shopping rounds.

The nature-lover is spoilt for choice in the countryside of Wessex. This is a land rich in birds, butterflies and animals occupying an enormous variety of habitats. Heathland, farmland, estuaries, rivers and unspoilt coastline shelter a vast array of creatures. The heathland of Dorset, though under pressure from developers, is home to British snakes and lizards, the Dartford warbler, and many colourful species of butterfly. There are important seabird colonies at several points on the Channel and an ancient colony of mute swans at Abbotsbury. Waders and wildfowl abound in the estuaries of the Severn and in Poole harbour. The flooded Somerset Levels act as a beacon to migrating Bewick's swans each winter and are a permanent home to snipe and curlew.

The woods which used to cover Wessex have now disappeared, even on Cranborne Chase which was once a forest. With them we have lost a number of traditional creatures, though one, the rare red squirrel, can still be found on the National Trust's Brownsea Island in Poole Harbour. In the present century the pressure on the countryside has increased, consuming precious heathland and hedgerows and firing a heated controversy over the ecology of the region.

Thomas Hardy

The English novelist Thomas Hardy (1840-1928) is largely responsible for the use of the term Wessex in modern Britain, though his definition of the 'kingdom' is as personal as any other. Hardy was born at Higher Bockhampton near Dorchester in a cottage now run by the National Trust. Dorset was the centre of both his fictional and personal worlds. The county resonates through his work in novels like *Far From the Madding Crowd, Under the Greenwood Tree, Return of the Native, Jude the Obscure* and *Tess of the d'Urbervilles.*

Hardy seemed destined to become no more than a competent town architect in Dorchester until he met his future wife Emma who persuaded him to concentrate upon writing. At the age of 30, he abandoned his profession and devoted himself to writing about the people, customs and countryside of his native land. He was famous by his mid-thirties, principally for *Far From the Madding Crowd.* Most of Hardy's life was spent in Dorchester, in the house he designed, Max Gate, a prolific novelist and later a poet of world renown. Max Gate is closed to the public but the writer's study has been recreated in the Dorset County Museum in Dorchester, with his library, the pens he used, and a calendar stopped at the day he died in January 1928.

Though Hardy's ashes lie in Poet's Corner at Westminster Abbey, his heart is buried in the churchyard at Stinsford. The author created a mythical kingdom of Wessex in which the familiar towns and villages around him reappeared lightly disguised, Dorchester transformed into Casterbridge and Oxford, which Hardy included in the eastern end of the region, renamed Christminster. A map drawn by the author delineates the transformation precisely and sets out the territory for virtually every one of his many tales.

The Wessex of Hardy is still recognisable today, and, with a good deal of research, it is possible for the Hardy lover to trace and retrace the locations of some of the famous scenes from the books. Hardy was acutely aware of the cultural and historical heritage of the area in which he lived. Old country customs, the ancient monuments of Wessex, and the geography of the land shape his characters and the tales which engulf them. Hardy, more than most writers, is indivisible from the countryside which produced him.

The Arthur Legends

The legend of King Arthur is a thread that runs throughout Wessex, and beyond into other parts of England and, on occasion, Europe. It is hard to take a step in that most Arthurian of destinations Glastonbury without coming across some reference to the tale, even if it is only Merlin's Wine Bar or the Camelot Tyre Centre.

It is a colourful tale, in all its myriad variations, and one that seems to strike a chord within the human imagination. The outline of the tale will be familiar... that of the boy who becomes king when he plucks the sword Excalibur from the stone. The Arthurian capital city of Camelot and the fellowship of the Round Table follow, the latter a brotherhood dedicated to righting wrongs through chivalrous conduct. The downfall of the Arthurian world begins with the fateful liaison between Arthur's favourite knight, Lancelot, and his queen, Guinevere. And ends on the battlefield with the forces of darkness, after which Arthur is mysteriously carried away, mortally wounded, to the far off Isle of Avalon, with the unspoken promise that he will return one day in England's hour of peril. Such is the stuff of poetry, novel, Disney cartoons and several cinema epics.

Arthur has spawned his own tourist industry and a vast collection of books which purport to tell his story, variously sorting truth from myth or, more often, injecting a touch more conjecture into a story which is already riddled with uncertainties. Several entire books have been devoted to dissecting the Arthurian legends, looking for clues in the distant Dark Ages which might shed some light on the shadowy hero, the once and future king. As with all works of mythology, it is those which claim to have identified the true Arthur which catch the imagination, and those which stick to historical truths which gather dust on the library shelves.

The question 'did Arthur exist?' is now a side issue, subsidiary to the greater enigma of the character's enduring popularity with generations of European readers. But, since it will be met with some frequency in many parts of Wessex, it should be tackled here briefly. The earliest references to a hero king called Arthur place him in Dark Ages Wales, fighting off the invading Saxons. This was a Celtic Arthur, active too in Curnow, the Cornish Celtic kingdom, but strangely absent in Wessex. For the Saxon and Celtic story-tellers Arthur was a malleable hero, forever willing to be translated into whatever form of nationalist was required for the society of the time. His entry into Wessex came at the end of the 12th century with the discovery of his 'grave' at Glastonbury, an event which was to transform the fortunes of the town and its monastery.

According to Geoffrey of Monmouth, whose *History of the Kings of Britain and Life of Merlin,* both spread the Arthur legend, the king had been mortally wounded at the battle of Camlan and conveyed to the mysterious Isle of Avalon where, in time, he was promised a return to full health. This confirmed one of the key aspects of the Arthur legend – that of the king who would rejoin his country's side at a future hour of need. But the Isle of Avalon was as much a puzzle to the reader of 900 years ago as it is to a modern follower of Arthur.

The monks of Glastonbury attempted to offer a solution, stating, simply, that the town had been known as the Isle of Avalon in earlier times, being surrounded by the marshes of the Somerset Levels. The appeal of this imagery will be instantly appreciated by the visitor who sees Glastonbury Tor surrounded by mist in the light of early morning, an eerie sight which seems perfect for the location of a local legend. Arthur's grave was discovered during the burial of a monk from the monastery. An ancient leaden cross conveniently named the king. There is a strong likelihood that the 'discovery' was no more than a simple deception by the monastery to attract free-spending pilgrims and support from the king and nobility (which it certainly did). Richard Barber's *The Figure of Arthur* (Longman, 1972) is a cool and lucid assessment of the Glastonbury myths which should be digested by any reader with a serious interest in the Arthur legends. Nevertheless, from that day in 1119 (or possibly 1191, accounts vary) when the mysterious oak coffin was uncovered, Glastonbury was unquestionably linked with the heroic king, and other parts of Wessex were to follow.

Cadbury Castle, in particular, laid claim to being the site of the original Camelot. Yet the very name Camelot was never attached to the Arthur story until Chrétien de Troyes's *Lancelot* in the late 12th century, and the author probably copied the name from Camulodunum, the Roman name for Colchester on the other side of the country. And Tintagel... no, the Arthur legends do not stand up to intense scrutiny. Their interest lies in the fascination they hold in many different languages and the body of literature and music which have been inspired by this shadowy figure of the Dark Ages, from Broadway's *Camelot* to the *Parsifal* of Wagner.

Food

Regional cuisine is virtually extinct in Britain, but Wessex remains notable for the quality and variety of its restaurants. Fresh produce is the basis of a good kitchen anywhere and in this part of the country the enthusiastic food lover can find good meat, fish and vegetables. Small fishing fleets are active all along the south coast, landing excellent, if sometimes expensive, crab, white fish and, in places, red mullet. Most seaside towns will place a particular emphasis on fresh fish, and, for an inexpensive traditional lunch, there is little to beat a fresh crab sandwich and a pint of Dorset bitter. A plate of assorted *fruits de mer* in one of Poole's more expensive harbourside restaurants can prove as memorable as any similar experience on the other side of the Channel.

Cheddar is, of course, famous for its cheese, and several manu-facturers in the region invite visitors to watch the cheesemaking process. The attachment of the name Cheddar to a packet of cheese is, of course, no guarantee that it was even made in Britain, least of all in Somerset. The ubiquitous 'cheddar' is now made in Ireland, Canada, America and New Zealand, as well as other parts of Britain. Frankly, it is stretching belief to insist that the Cheddar of Somerset is best of all. Certainly, very good Cheddar can be found in Wessex, as can some fine local goat cheese specialities. But the quality of cheese is more to do with the skill of its makers and the way in which it is kept than its place of origin. Specialist cheese shops do flourish in several Wessex towns, Glastonbury and Shaftesbury among them, and are well worth visiting. A pint of good cider, a Wessex apple and a slice of local Cheddar makes for a good Somerset lunch... but the plate is less appetising if the glass is filled from a homogenous supermarket bottle and the cheese is the plastic foreign variety which, incomprehensibly, is as popular with the pubs of Wessex as it is with those of other parts of the country.

The meat industry of Britain is now almost completely national, so it is difficult to discern much in the way of local trends in the beef, pork and lamb of Wessex. Excellent little butchers flourish in many parts, and you will still find a few who bake their own pies and cook their own hams. Game and wildfowl frequently appear on the menus of the more expensive restaurants but these are usually bought in from national markets, though none the less delicious for that.

Drink

The most famous drink of this part of Britain is cider, a beverage more ancient than its more popular counterpart, beer. First class cider can still be found in parts of Somerset today, though much of the industry has fallen victim to rationalisation and the mass production of bland, supermarket brands. Cider has been made in all parts of Britain where apples are grown commercially, Kent, Suffolk, Herefordshire and Dorset among them. But it is in Somerset where the cidermaker's art is at its best, producing a drink that is as sophisticated and individual to the region as any French vineyard classification.

West Country cider originated on the farm, not in the brewhouse. It was made each autumn by individual farmers for personal consumption, for sale to local inns and as a working allowance for farm labourers. It was not unusual for farmworkers to be allowed as much as four pints a day in free cider in reward for labour in the fields.

What sets Somerset apart from other cidermaking areas is the kind of apple used. Many areas, including Normandy and the eastern counties of Britain, will happily make cider from whatever dessert or cooking apples are available. Cox's and Bramleys provide the staple juice for much of the cider seen on supermarket shelves today. To the true cider lover, this is like trying to make champagne from the same grapes sold on a greengrocer's counter. Just as the brewing industry cultivated several kinds of hop for their individual flavours, cidermakers established different strains of apple purely for the production of cider. These varieties, with colourful names such as Brown Snout, Strawberry Norman, Dymock Red, Foxwhelp, Cider Lady's Finger and Skyrme's Kernel, tend to fall into two categories, bittersweets and bittersharps. Much of the cidermaker's art depends upon the ratio of bittersweets to bittersharps used to press the juice before fermentation. Similar variations occur in pear trees used to produce perry, increasingly rare even in West Country pubs except in the homogenised versions disguised as sparkling white wine.

Since the war, many acres of traditional cider varieties have been grubbed out and replaced with standard dessert trees or cookers such as Bramley which can double for both cider and general sale. The producers argue that this is the result of a changing public taste towards lighter, sweeter cider. The truth is that the changes were more part of a marketing campaign by the big producers designed to produce mass-market cider brands recognisable in High Street retail outlets. It was a tactic that worked, and transformed some of the older, larger cider firms, but at the expense of more traditional, smaller producers. Nevertheless, the visitor to Wessex can often find real farmhouse cider in local freehouses. A sure sign is a group of locals inspecting a slightly cloudy pale pint drawn from a barrel behind the counter.

The cidermaking process is complex and more highly skilled than, perhaps, one might expect. After picking, the fruit is often allowed to lie undisturbed for several weeks before milling. The crushed fruit is then pressed into a 'cheese', a core of pulp, often kept in place by straw in traditional methods, from which the last amounts of juice are extracted. After pressing, the juice is transferred into casks where natural yeasts start the fermentation process. Commercial cidermakers are more scientific and may well add their own, specially prepared, yeasts to control the process. After fermentation in the barrel over winter, the cider is ready for drinking by the following spring. Commercial cider is produced more quickly and rarely aged.

There are many variations which can alter the final quality of the cider during the fermentation process. Some producers will use wooden barrels previously used to hold sherry or rum which pass on the flavour of the original contents. The cider can also be racked to remove some of its natural cloudiness. During bottling, small amounts of sugar can be added to produce a secondary fermentation which will make the cider effervescent (the drink is, in its natural state, quite still). There is as much variation available to the expert cidermaker as there is for the master winemaker. A smooth, strong apple wine, backed with a hint of dry sherry, a deep tan pint of aromatic pub cider clear to the bottom of the glass, or a more traditional drink clouded by the juice from the original pressing... all are determined by the choice of apple and processing.

The term 'scrumpy' is one frequently used for farmhouse 'rough' cider sold in West Country pubs. It should be approached with some care. True scrumpy is usually poor quality cider from an amateur producer, often badly fermented, sour and dangerously strong. Farmhouse cider from a good producer, while still more acid than retail brands, is a different creature altogether, rich in flavours and aromas while, if taken in moderation, kind to the system the day after. Sheppy's Cider Farm, at Bradford-on-Tone near Taunton, is a good place to see traditional cidermaking. The farm has 42 acres of cider orchards, a museum of old cidermaking equipment, and is run by a family which has been involved in the production of cider for nearly 200 years. (Open Monday to Saturday all year, Sundays 12 noon to 2pm from Easter to Christmas, tel: 0823 461233). Other, smaller cider farms welcome visitors periodically; inquire at local tourist information centres for details.

English winemakers are also beginning to make their home in Wessex. Usually they will be producing light, Germanic wines of estate-bottled quality, since this is the type of vintage most suited to the English climate. Prices tend to be fairly high, principally because of the small scale of production compared with the large winemaking industry of Europe. Due to EEC regulations, all English wine must be classified as table wine; there is no appellation contrôlée designation for Britain. The better English wines are certainly of a higher quality than this, however, and would, in Germany, have attracted a more select classification.

The drink of Thomas Hardy was beer, and Wessex remains a part of England blessed with a good selection of traditional breweries. The number of pubs which lay claim to the patronage of the great writer defies record. The beer that Hardy knew was 'real ale', true English bitter, uncarbonated, stored in barrels, and served through handpumps, and the names with which he was familiar remain in business today.

In his home town of Dorchester Eldridge Pope produce a strong bottled ale named after the author and an equally robust bitter, Royal Oak. Devenish, which grew up in Weymouth and still has its offices there, no longer brews in Dorset, but look out for the smaller Palmers of Bridport and Hall and Woodhouse of Blandford. Wiltshire has one of the great British brewers in Arkells of Swindon, frequently seen as guest beer in a variety of tied houses, while Courage's Bristol headquarters produces excellent best and the heavy, tasty Director's. All real ales depend upon a landlord or landlady's skills for their quality, since they must be kept correctly, in spotless conditions, and served in prime condition. Sadly this can be relied on no more in Wessex than elsewhere.

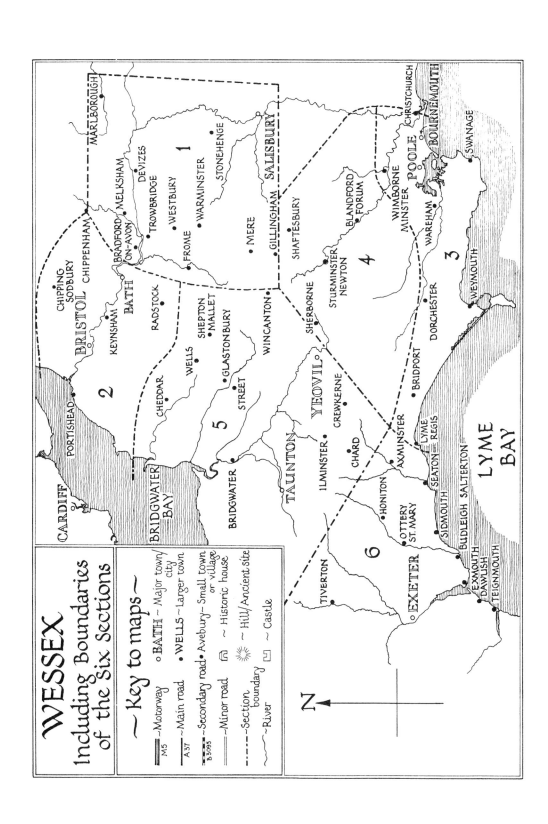

WESSEX
Including Boundaries
of the Six Sections

~ Key to maps ~

M5 ~ Motorway	o BATH ~ Major town/ city
A.37 ~ Main road	• WELLS ~ Larger town
B 3095 ~ Secondary road	• Avebury ~ Small town or village
~ Minor road	⌂ ~ Historic house
---- ~ Section boundary	☼ ~ Hill/Ancient site
~ River	⌷ ~ Castle

N

CARDIFF

BRISTOL
CHIPPING SODBURY
CHIPPENHAM
KEYNSHAM
RADSTOCK
BATH
BRADFORD ON-AVON
MELKSHAM
TROWBRIDGE
DEVIZES
MARLBOROUGH
WESTBURY
FROME
WARMINSTER
STONEHENGE

1

2

PORTISHEAD

BRIDGWATER BAY

CHEDDAR
WELLS
SHEPTON MALLET
GLASTONBURY
STREET

5

BRIDGWATER

TAUNTON

WINCANTON
MERE
GILLINGHAM
SHAFTESBURY
SALISBURY

SHERBORNE
STURMINSTER NEWTON
BLANDFORD FORUM
WIMBORNE MINSTER

4

POOLE
CHRISTCHURCH
BOURNEMOUTH
SWANAGE

YEOVIL
CREWKERNE
ILMINSTER
CHARD

WAREHAM
WEYMOUTH

3

DORCHESTER

BRIDPORT
LYME REGIS
AXMINSTER
SEATON
BUDLEIGH SALTERTON

LYME BAY

TIVERTON

6

HONITON
OTTERY ST. MARY
SIDMOUTH
EXMOUTH
DAWLISH
TEIGNMOUTH

EXETER

Traveller's Information

BY CAR

The M3 motorway is a fast and easy route into the north of the region. The M5 runs to the west as far as Exeter, while the M3 and M27 offer reasonably reliable access to the east via the A31. All routes into Wessex become busy at weekends and on bank holidays; the M5 is a particularly notorious blackspot for traffic jams and should be avoided whenever possible during sunny public holidays.

PUBLIC TRANSPORT

There are reasonable, and occasionally excellent, train services to all the major towns and cities of the area, but it is difficult to see much of the more remote countryside by public transport. Bus passes are available which offer inexpensive rural travel if you have the time, but be sure to plan your itinerary carefully since services are limited in the quieter parts of the area.

WALKING

There is now an established public footpath running the length of the south west coast, from the Isle of Purbeck near Poole to Land's End. The Wessex sections are the Dorset Coastal Path and the Devon South Coast Path. Shorter, local walks are noted in the relevant local sections.

ACCOMMODATION

Wessex has largely escaped the process of 'Fortefication' which has seen the traditional large hotels of England engulfed by various somewhat characterless mass chains. There are some splendid individual hotels in the area, including some of the best luxury category establishments in Britain, Ston Easton Hall and the Castle at Taunton among them. In addition, there is a broad range of less expensive private hotels of good quality, some of them, such as Glastonbury's historic George and Pilgrims, as interesting architecturally as they are delightful to visit. There is a wide selection of bed and breakfast accommodation through-out the West Country, much of it consisting of comfortable rooms in elegant private homes.

Almost all tourist information offices in the area offer an accommodation booking service, often with pictures of the properties concerned, and it is possible to find some excellent bargains in this way. But do not expect to be able to find rooms in the best establishments at short notice during the peak weeks of summer or at weekends.

WEEKEND AND SHORT BREAKS

The range of discounted offers available to couples and families who are travelling on short or weekend breaks is too great to document. Almost all hotels will offer winter break discounts; many have them running throughout the year. These can be very reasonable ways to sample expensive hotels which would normally be thought impossibly dear. Virtually all these discounts do involve dinner in the hotel, however, and, in some of the chain establishments, this is distinctly less interesting than might be found in a private restaurant elsewhere. You may find it instructive to compare the price of the weekend with the discount against the normal price; in some cases the difference is scarcely worth the trouble of locking yourself into dining in the hotel. All hotels will offer you a discount against long stays of a week or more; inquire direct of the owner.

Most of the entries in the private accommodation here are somewhat above the basic B&B level. Several are in lovely, historic houses which reserve a few rooms for paying guests and serve excellent home cooking to boot. A number of such premises throughout the country are now members of a joint marketing organisation, Wolsey Lodges (17 Chapel Street, Bildeston, Suffolk IP7 7EP, tel: 0449 741297) which publishes an annual guide to members' houses. It is highly recommended.

RATINGS

Each accommodation entry has been given a rating of up to four stars. This is a measure of price, not of quality. All of the premises listed here are thought to be worth visiting. The star rating is designed to give you a comparative indication of cost.

Stonehenge, Wiltshire

1 Salisbury, Marlborough, Avebury and Stonehenge

The city of Salisbury is best known for its magnificent cathedral and associated Close. There is an attractive city centre with characterful old streets and buildings and a walk to Old Sarum, the original site of the town. To the north, across Salisbury Plain, lies the lovely old town of Marlborough and around it some of the most ancient monuments of Britain: the prehistoric stones of Stonehenge and Avebury and the mysterious Silbury Hill. Salisbury is an excellent base for the area, with a good range of hotels and restaurants. A weekend is ample time for visiting the principal sights.

Salisbury

It is impossible to dislike Salisbury, a cathedral city of great beauty and individual character. Yet the city we know today is, by comparison with some of its neighbours, relatively modern.

The original Salisbury was Sarum, two miles to the north on a chilly chalk hill defended by a ditch. Now known as Old Sarum, it had been occupied since pre-Roman times and was briefly the site of an important Norman castle and cathedral of which only ruins now remain. William the Conqueror reviewed his forces there in 1070, four years after his famous invasion, and gave his blessing to the site's development as both spiritual and military centre for the region. But soldiers and priests rarely agreed on Old Sarum, and the bleakness of the hill led to growing complaints from the clergy who were pressing for a new, more comfortable home out of reach of the military. The modern visitor, walking around the bleak ramparts on a windy day, will well understand the unhappiness of the priests. In the early 13th century, their grievances were investigated by a representative of Pope Honorius III, so seriously were they taken. The report spoke of a church shaken by wind and storm, far removed from a good water supply, and oppressed by the castle military who placed obstacles in the way of leaving and entering the enclosure. By 1219, after a brawl between the two camps, the clergy had decided to move.

Colourful stories surround the selection of present-day Salisbury as the site of the new city. Some claim that an arrow was fired into the sky from Old Sarum and the spot where it landed chosen for the new cathedral. Others say the place was suggested to the Bishop Richard Poore in a dream. Whatever the truth, the new site made much more sense to the civilian population, since it was fertile, well watered and easily supplied. On April 28, 1220, work began on a new cathedral for the new city and one of England's most famous sights began to take shape.

New Sarum soon eclipsed its older neighbour which rapidly declined in stature, becoming first a castle then a prison. Today, the hill is covered with the scattered ruins of the old settlement and makes a good place to begin a visit to the area. The walk from the centre of Salisbury to Old Sarum takes under an hour and covers about five miles there and back. From the centre of town, follow the footpath on the west side of the River Avon, past the Boathouse pub, under the dual carriageway of Churchill Way West and then cross the river, turning immediately left. Here another footpath leads through playing fields and allotments. Turn right after the allotments to reach Stratford Road, continue out of the city then turn sharp right towards the hill of Old Sarum.

In the hedge along this path stands the Parliament Stone, a reminder of the days of Old Sarum as a rotten borough. When parliamentary seats could be bought and sold, Old Sarum retained its right to elect an MP even though the borough had only a handful of residents. The system became infamous during the 18th century and was eventually stamped out by the Reform Act of 1832 which abolished Old Sarum, along with 55 other rotten boroughs. The stone marks the spot where the returning

Close Gate, Salisbury

officer of the election sat under an elm tree to count the parliamentary vote – since there was no building in the constituency which could be used for the purpose.

Even in ruins Old Sarum is a magnificent spectacle, composed of two perfectly circular earthworks, one within the other. The arrangement dates from prehistoric times and was adopted by everyone who succeeded to the windy hill, Iron Age man, sophisticated Roman, untutored Saxon. In the outer ring lie the remains of the Norman cathedral, with the ground plan still clearly visible, uncovered through patient excavation work begun in Victorian times. In the inner part of the hill lie traces of the last inhabited parts of the settlement, the palace of the bishop, an undercroft, a kitchen and the original gatehouse at the heart of the fortification. You can retrace your steps to Salisbury along the same route or take another path, behind the Old Castle Restaurant, which eventually reaches St Mark's Avenue and Churchill Way North, a few yards from the centre of the city.

Salisbury Cathedral

The sudden departure of the clerics of Old Sarum to the new city of Salisbury determined the nature of the new cathedral. Virtually every cathedral in Britain has taken more than a century, sometimes several, to complete and is consequently a mixture of different, occasionally conflicting, styles. Salisbury appeared in one constant burst of enthusiasm on an open site. Nothing had to be incorporated from the past, nothing was to encroach in the future. Only 38 years after the service to mark the start of construction in 1220, the structure – save the magnificent spire – was complete. It is this homogeneity which makes it unique; the style used throughout is the variation of Gothic known as Early English.

The cathedral stands in its own magnificent Close, the largest in England, forming a separate, picturesque community behind the main entrance of the High Street Gate. This was the heart of New Sarum, and the houses around the cathedral are the original homes of the clerical community which ruled the city. The lovely Chapter House on the south side, attached to the cathedral cloisters, was the administrative centre of the original community. Behind walls built from the rubble of Old Sarum, protected by the portcullis which once protected the High Street Gate, Salisbury flourished under the rule of bishops.

The Close and the cathedral must rank among the great city sights of England and can, for the dedicated, absorb several days. Here there is only space for a compressed description of the principal sights which greet the visitor on passing through the High Street Gate. The cathedral is the obvious first stop on any visit to Salisbury, but it merits an external examination before stepping through the main doors. From outside, the visitor can appreciate the completeness of the single style of architecture used in the building and the majesty of the great spire. Added in 1334, it soars 404 feet above ground, about five times the height of the main ceiling. Impressive as the spire is, it has posed many problems. Sir Christopher Wren declared the structure unsound. The spire was 23 inches out of alignment, and the cathedral itself built on shifting and uncertain ground. Expensive stabilising work has been carried out and more will be necessary. An appeal to raise funds for the spire was launched in 1985 by the Prince of Wales.

The cathedral is entered through the west door and immediately reveals an impressive view of the entire interior, with its forest of columns and gentle arches. The recommended route around the building begins along the left of the nave. This passes the medieval clock, built in 1386, which is thought to be the oldest working clock in the world, and the north door with glass panels by Laurence Whistler. Among the medieval tombs is that of 'giant' Sir John Cheney who was unhorsed by Richard III in the fateful battle of Bosworth. The knight was aptly named; from his skeleton it is estimated he was about seven feet tall. Standing underneath the spire it is possible to see how the supporting pillars have bent under the strain of the 6,500 tons of stone above them.

Walk past the ornate 19th-century wooden choir. To the left is a memorial stone to one Thomas Lambert 'BORNE MAY YE 14 AN DO 1783 & DYED FEB 19 the same year'. This seemingly impossible feat of dying before you are born is explained by a change in the calendar during 1783. On the north side is the small Morning Chapel with a 13th-century screen. At the western end of the cathedral lies the earliest part of the building, the Trinity Chapel. Returning on the south side of the building, the visitor reaches the ornate tomb of a family of local gentry, the Mompessons, burial place of Sir Richard Mompesson and thought to be the finest tomb in the cathedral. Leave the nave to the south to find the cloisters, the largest in Britain and unusual in a place which has never functioned as a monastery.

The Chapter House leads off the cloisters to the east and is, for many, the high point of any visit to the cathedral. The lovely octagonal hall has, at its centre, a delicately carved pillar which reaches 52 feet to the ceiling. All around the walls are intricate carvings depicting biblical scenes; the 60 groups taken together form one of the great masterpieces of 13th-century sculpture, though the name of the artist is not known. In the Chapter House too is one of the four remaining original copies of the Magna Carta, written in 76 lines of script on a single skin. Two other copies are in the British Museum and one is in Lincoln Cathedral.

The Cathedral Close

Mompesson House, now owned by the National Trust, King's House, the home of the Salisbury and South Wiltshire Museum, and the Duke of Edinburgh's Royal Regimental Museum are the three sights demanding the visitor's attention most in the Close. Mompesson House was built in 1701 and, for 97 years, was the home of the Victorian artist Barbara Townsend. It was later used as the residence of the Bishop of Salisbury before being donated to the National Trust in 1952. The interior rooms have suffered little alteration over the last century and there is an interesting collection of furniture, paintings and an exhibition of 18th-century drinking glasses.

King's House is one of the best museums in the region, housed in a 13th-century building which was originally the home of the Abbot of Sherborne. Richard III is said to have stayed in the house when the Duke of Buckingham, a former supporter who betrayed him, was captured in Shrewsbury. The unfortunate duke was conveyed to Salisbury by the King's men and unceremoniously beheaded in the yard of the Blue Boar Inn in the Market Square. Local folklore says that the severed head was brought to King's House for Richard III to see. The name of the house is thought to come from the occupancy of James Sadler, a friend of James I who played host to the monarch several times. It was later a college until the advent of the museum in 1981. There are interesting and highly informative displays on the history of Stonehenge, which merits a whole gallery, the development of Salisbury and ceramics galleries. Among the folk exhibits are the figures of the 14-foot Salisbury giant and Hob-nob, a hobby horse, used in pageants during the 15th and 16th centuries. The figures, operated from within by one man, were a popular part of the annual fairs which could once be seen throughout the West Country.

31

The Duke of Edinburgh's Royal Regimental Museum is housed in the regimental headquarters, the 15th-century mansion known as The Wardrobe – it was once used for storing clerical clothes – on the west of the Close. The regiment is a modern one, formed in 1959, but with ancient origins. It was created from the Royal Berkshire Regiment and the Wiltshire Regiment which both have antecedents going back three centuries. The museum documents action by the regiment and its forebears all over the world, from Jamaica to China. One of the more unusual exhibits is a stuffed mongrel, Bobby, wearing the Afghan Campaign Medal. The dog, a sergeant's pet, escaped the massacre at Maiwand in 1880 during the Second Afghan Wars and, in spite of a bad bullet wound, followed the 11 surviving soldiers of the ambushed Berkshire brigade to safety. Queen Victoria presented the dog with the campaign medal when the regiment returned to England. The story has a rather bleak ending; the dog was run over and killed by a hackney cab two years after its triumphant return to England.

There remains much of interest beyond the Close. St Thomas's Church, in St Thomas's Square, is as old as the cathedral itself. Its most startling possession is a 15th-century 'Doom painting' a depiction of the end of the world, which covers the whole of the chancel arch. The work is a pure piece of horror fiction designed to instil fear in the illiterate incapable of reading the Bible. A variety of sinners are dragged to their doom by assorted demons, while the worthy walk from their graves to heaven and the figure of Christ surveys the scene from on high. Such paintings were once common in English churches, though they were rarely so large. St Thomas's was whitewashed in Elizabethan times and remained covered until the early 19th century. The Victorians later removed all the whitewash and made an attempt at restoration with oil paint.

Salisbury rewards the aimless wanderer. There are interesting old buildings – houses, shops, pubs and hotels – in many of the ancient streets of the city centre, around the old market place, which has been used since the 13th century, and beyond. Butcher Row, Fish Row, Blue Boar Row and Silver Street all reflect their heritage in name and, to varying degrees, appearance. The city is also famous for its friendly old pubs, of which none is better than the Haunch of Venison in Minster Street opposite the Poultry Cross, a small landmark which was once the place where poultry was sold in the medieval city. The Haunch of Venison is a narrow 14th-century inn with a characterful wooden interior and a lively local clientele. How it survived the gentrification

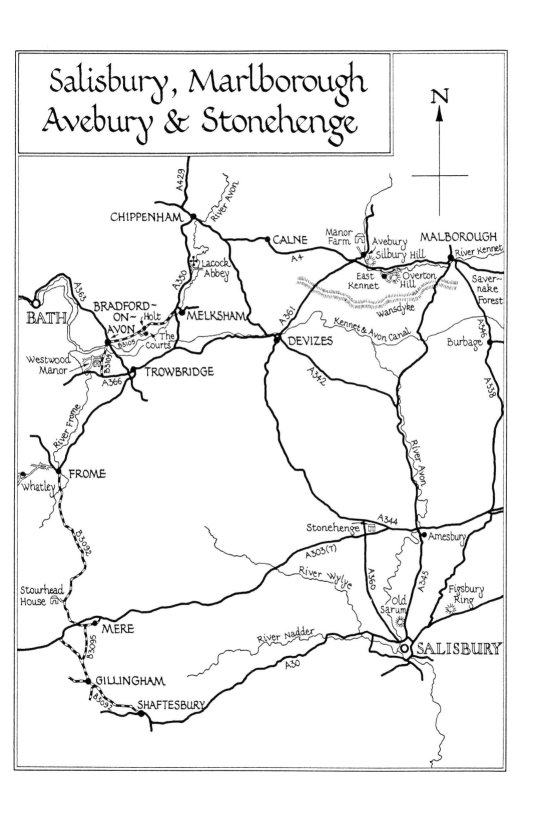

Salisbury, Marlborough Avebury & Stonehenge

N

CHIPPENHAM

A429

River Avon

CALNE

A4

Manor Farm

Avebury
Silbury Hill

MALBOROUGH

River Kennet

Lacock Abbey

A350

East Kennet

Overton Hill

Saver-nake Forest

A363

BRADFORD~ON~AVON

Holt

MELKSHAM

A361

Wansdyke

A346

BATH

The Courts

B5109

Kennet & Avon Canal

DEVIZES

Burbage

Westwood Manor

A366

TROWBRIDGE

A342

A338

River Frome

River Avon

FROME

Whatley

Stonehenge

A344

A303(T)

Amesbury

A345

B3092

River Wylye

A360

Figsbury Ring

Stourhead House

Old Sarum

MERE

B3095

River Nadder

SALISBURY

B3092

GILLINGHAM

A30

SHAFTESBURY

inflicted on similar premises elsewhere is a mystery, but it is surely worth a visit, even for the curious teetotaller.

Stonehenge

The most impressive Bronze Age monument in the world lies 10 miles north of Salisbury, close to Amesbury. This is a part of Britain haunted by the presence of prehistoric man. As an earlier writer, the archeologist Jacquetta Hawkes, author of the classic *Guide to the Prehistoric and Roman Monuments of England and Wales*, puts it: 'Wessex is the core and propelling heart of the whole of prehistoric Britain away from the highland country'. The map hereabouts is dotted with the tell-tale relics of ancient man, long barrows, burial mounds, hill encampments and earthworks so numerous that they supply the raw material for a veritable industry of archeology. Nearby lies the massive Figsbury Ring, a 15-acre Iron Age hill fort. Further north is the ancient complex of Avebury.

There is a sense of mystery about many of these monuments which has captured the imagination of visitors, and none so much as magical Stonehenge. The monument comprises bluestone and sarsen stones within an encircling ditch and bank. This baffling stone circle has attracted scholars, mystics and cranks for centuries and will doubtless continue to do so for centuries to come. Yet in all honesty, no-one can say with any certainty why the precisely-built stone circle was erected or what purpose it served. This has not prevented speculation, of course, and it is not hard to find, in the more obscure bookshops of Glastonbury, works which set out to prove that Stonehenge was a landing pad for extra terrestrials, the headquarters of a sacrificial druidic cult or something even more bizarre. The riddle of Stonehenge is great fun but it is perfectly insoluble.

What do we know for certain about Stonehenge? One unassailable fact is that the structure had no historic connection whatsoever with the Celtic sect of the Druids, though today they are its best known visitors. Each Midsummer Day modern Druids travel to the stones to celebrate the solstice, an event which, in recent years, has been clouded by antagonism between police and hippie convoys intent on joining the event. The spell of Stonehenge does not diminish with the years, however tenuous the original connection. The earliest construction on the site probably dates from around 3,000 BC. The prehistoric 'cathedral'

– for it seems fairly certain that the site had some kind of ceremonial or religious significance – was added to and altered over the next two millennia, and was at the height of its use some 1,500 years before the birth of Christ. There *may* be reason to believe that a craftsman from ancient Greece was involved in its construction, since there is evidence of contact between Mycenae and the men of Wessex, but this is largely conjecture.

There is no doubt that the structure represents a considerable feat of engineering for such a primitive society. The simple task of bringing the great stones to Stonehenge must have been taxing – the bluestones came from Pembrokeshire, the great sarsens from the Marlborough Downs. Furthermore, it is patently clear that the site was constructed to celebrate the Midsummer Solstice, probably as part of a religious festival. It is very precisely located so that the axis of principal stones aligns with the sun on this day each year, and there are other geometric arrangements in the layout of the stones which point to an advanced astronomical understanding on the part of the scheme's creators. The modern scientist and astronomer, Sir Fred Hoyle, is adamant that Stonehenge could only have been built by a civilisation with a profound and accurate understanding of both astronomy and mathematics.

Certainly, this was an important and revered monument in the ancient kingdom of Wessex. Did ancient man find his way to Stonehenge in much the same way that the modern pilgrim travels to St Peter's in Rome? There is a lot to be said for the idea. The site continues to exert its powers today. It is too famous, of course, and forever populated by camera-wielding visitors of all nationalities. This very pressure on the stones has forced the authorities to introduce control systems which have an unfortunate 20th-century brusqueness about them: concrete car parks, uniformed staff, entry and exit signs strictly enforced. But for all this it is impossible to stand among the stones themselves and not feel a sense of wonder and puzzlement about their origins and the ancient people behind them.

Marlborough

Let us leave ancient Britain, if only for a little while. Marlborough has its mysteries – there is a mound in the grounds of the famous college of the town which is said to be the resting place of Arthur's wayward magician, Merlin – but the place's pleasures belong to the current millennium.

This is a small, handsome country town of genteel nature. The great, wide High Street lies on the old coaching route from Bath to London. In the heady days of Regency Bath, it was a popular break in the journey from London for the fashionable travellers going west. Kings drawn to the area, for sport in Savernake, often stayed in the castle which once occupied the site of today's college. The diarist Pepys knew Marlborough well and described the terrible fire of 1653 which destroyed much of the High Street. To the south east is Savernake Forest, once a royal hunting ground, now lovely walking country. South of the town runs Wansdyke, the remains of a defensive wall for Wessex built during the dark and dangerous days which followed the collapse of the Roman empire. There is a white horse in the chalk a little way out of town, too, but it is relatively modern, carved in the last century by pupils of the college.

Kingsbury Street, Marlborough

Today the town is less hurried, a place of genteel shops, interesting narrow alleys, and the splendid thoroughfare of the High Street, with its happy mixture of architectural styles, from 17th-century timber frames to Regency bow windows. There are two churches. St Mary's, opposite the town hall, was badly damaged in the fire and partly rebuilt. Inside, let into the wall, are fragments of Roman sculptures, two grotesque heads and a figure of the goddess Fortuna holding a horn of plenty. The doorway under the west tower is Norman. St Peter's, near the college, has a handsome 120 foot tower.

Avebury

Avebury is a prehistoric monument combined with a living village of considerable charm. To the professionals, it poses even more problems than Stonehenge; the visitor will find it equally as fascinating. As long ago as 1663 John Aubrey claimed Avebury 'does as much exceed Stonehenge in greatness as a cathedral does a parish church', but, then again, he was one of the place's most ardent publicists to the academic world.

Much of the village stands inside the ancient circle which enclosed nearly 29 acres behind bank and ditch. Village church, manor house and pub thrive in picture postcard fashion here, barely moved by the visitors who trek through daily in their hundreds. The comparison with Stonehenge is inevitable. There is an avenue of sarsens from the south leading to the centre of the village where two smaller circles can be found. The purpose of it all is beyond the wit of modern man, but it is certainly moving, particularly early on a misty morning in spring or autumn, before the crowds of coaches have started to arrive. Avebury is best visited early or late: in the middle of the day, particularly in summer, it can become uncomfortably crowded.

Outside the circle stands the greatest mystery, Silbury Hill, the largest man-made mound in Europe, 1,660 feet round at the base and 130 feet high. There have been several excavations at Silbury, the most recent in 1968/9 carried out by the BBC in conjunction with archeologists. But the promise of great finds was never rewarded; all the dig unearthed was a pot containing a Victorian Bible poster, placed there during a previous dig in 1849. The BBC dig seems to have ended any theory that Silbury was constructed as a tomb, an idea that had been prevalent locally for centuries. Pepys, visiting the area in 1668, was told that the hill was called

'Selbury, from one King Seall buried there, as tradition says'. The theorists continue their work, and in recent years it has been suggested by one writer that the hill is a monument to the Great Goddess common to most prehistoric civilisations, and was part of an elaborate ceremony each Lammas Eve.

Silbury clearly played an important part in the ritual life of the inhabitants of ancient Avebury, but we shall probably never know precisely what. The face of this prehistoric community can be discerned, however. An avenue of stones ran from Overton Hill in the south east to the Avebury circle. Most of the stones used in Avebury have been purloined over the centuries for practical building work, but several have been unearthed and reset. It is a pleasant walk of some six miles from the village, first to Silbury, then to West Kennett, site of an excavated Long Barrow burial chamber, and finally to Overton Hill. Return by the road or the footpath to Manor Farm; both ways lead past stones and earthworks.

The village itself, encircled by its prehistoric ditch, has a good pub, the Red Lion, and a museum devoted to the finds of the Victorian archeologist Alexander Keiller who was the first to make a serious attempt to unravel the mysteries of Avebury. The church is interesting too, with Saxon windows and Norman features, a more comfortable place of worship than the prehistoric circles, without doubt, but one which is some three millennia younger.

Avebury Stones

Tourist Information

(* denotes a seasonal service only)

Fish Row
Salisbury
Tel: 0722 334956

St Peter's Church
High Street
Marlborough*
Tel: 0672 53989

The Great Barn
Avebury*
Tel: 06273 425

Hotels

New Inn
41/43 New Street
Salisbury
Wilts
Tel: 0722 27679
No smoking pub, hotel and restaurant, in
a handsome 15th-century building with
garden close to the cathedral. Highly
recommended.
Rooms: 8
Credit cards: Access, Visa, Amex, Diners
Rating ***

White Hart
1 St John Street
Salisbury
Wilts
Tel: 0722 27476
THF-run large coaching inn centrally
located.
Rooms: 68
Credit cards: Access, Visa, Amex, Diners
Rating ****

Private Accommodation

The Chantry
Church Street
Mere
Wilts
Tel: 0747 860264
Lovely 15th-century house with large
lake on the edge of Salisbury Plain.
Rooms: 3
Credit cards: none
Rating **

The Old Vicarage
Burbage
Marlborough
Wilts
Tel: 0672 810495
Victorian rectory south of Marlborough
on the edge of Savernake forest.
Rooms: 3
Credit cards: Access, Visa
Rating ***

Restaurants

New Inn
41/43 New Street
Salisbury
Tel: 0722 27679
Excellent home cooking – steaks, fish,
chicken and vegetarian dishes. No
smoking establishment.
Credit cards: Access, Visa, Amex, Diners
Rating ***

Haunch of Venison
1 Minster Street
Salisbury
Tel: 0722 22024
Traditional English cooking, with game
and more adventurous dishes, in first
floor restaurant of historic and
atmospheric pub.
Credit cards: Access, Visa
Rating ***

Manuel's
14 Ox Row
Market Place
Salisbury
Tel: 0722 28923
French cooking in popular restaurant
overlooking the Market Square.
Closed Mondays
Credit cards: Access, Visa
Rating ***

Harper's
The Market Square
Salisbury
Tel: 0722 333118
Adventurous modern cuisine with
continental and nouvelle leanings. Fixed
price menus available for lunch and
dinner.
Closed Sundays
Credit cards: Access, Visa
Rating ****

Historic Houses

Lacock Abbey (NT)
Lacock
3m S Chippenham
Magnificent abbey founded in 1232,
private home in the same family since
16th century. Barn houses museum
dedicated to the photographic pioneer
William Henry Fox Talbot. House March
to November 2-5.30, closed Tuesdays.
Cloisters, grounds and Fox Talbot
Museum of Photography March to
November 2-5.30 daily.

Mompesson House (NT)
Cathedral Close
Salisbury
Built in 1701 and the only private house in
the Close open to the public. Excellent
furniture collection and pretty walled
garden. March to November 12.30-5.30,
closed Thursdays and Fridays.

Stourhead House
3m NW Mere
Palladian mansion with Chippendale
furniture set in 2,500 acres of estate.
March to November 2-5.30 Sunday to
Wednesday; May to September also
Thursdays 2-5.30

Westwood Manor (NT)
Westwood
Bradford-on-Avon
Tudor stone manor house with extensive
antique furniture collection.
March to September, Sunday and
Monday 2-5.

Ancient Monuments

Avebury Stone Circle (NT)
Avebury
Megalithic monument composed of a 28-
acre site of stone circles approached by
an avenue of megaliths. Open daily all
year.

Old Sarum
Salisbury
Prehistoric earthworks and ruins of
Norman settlement that preceded
Salisbury. Summer 10-6, daily; rest of year
10-4, closed Mondays.

Stonehenge
Salisbury Plain
World famous Bronze Age Monument.
Daily ex. Sunday mornings, October to
March.

Gardens

The Courts (NT)
Holt
Nr Trowbridge
Exotic seven acres of gardens
surrounding private 18th-century house.
March to Oct 2-4.30, closed Sat.

View across Bath

2 Bath and Bristol

Roman city, fashionable Georgian resort, modern tourist attraction, Bath is a perennial item on the itinerary of travellers both foreign and domestic. The town has a busy cultural life and a popular annual arts festival. Bristol is a vibrant commercial city with an attractive central quarter based around the docks and the lovely suburb of Clifton on the Avon Gorge, crossed by Brunel's famous Suspension Bridge. Bath and Bristol are only 30 minutes apart by car. The former will appeal to those who wish to follow a more conventional tourist route – Bath is full of visitors all year round and depends upon them for its livelihood. Bristol is a more conventional and multi-faceted community, but there are fewer central hotels. The fast M4 motorway is the obvious route into the area for most people. But don't forget the original path of the old Bristol-London coach route, the A4, which is now relatively uncongested. It passes through several interesting areas of Wiltshire, and offers the chance to visit Marlborough and Avebury (see pp. 35-8) en route. Bath and Bristol can engulf as much time as the visitor has to spare: a weekend for each or both cities, or five days for a more leisurely stroll around their many sights. Weekend visitors take note: Sundays here are as sleepy as anywhere else in the British Isles and not the time to plan on much active sightseeing.

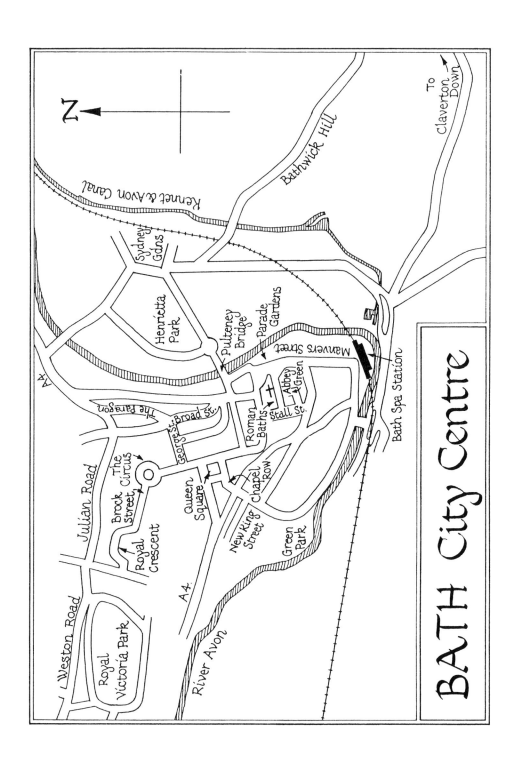

BATH City Centre

Bath

Three hot mineral springs provide the source of all Bath's considerable fame. They appear on the present site of the Pump Room and Roman Baths but predate man, the result of a unique geological formation which brings hot mineral water, at a constant temperature of 46° Centigrade, to the surface of the earth rain or shine. The spring in the King's Bath of the Pump Room produces a quarter of a million gallons a day alone and has done so for as long as man has populated Britain. Small wonder that the site has, over the millennia, gained a special place in the superstitions of those who inhabited the country.

The Romans, for whom bathing was a social and medicinal custom, arrived in the area shortly after the invasion of AD 43 and found a lively Celtic tradition which gave the stewardship of the springs to the goddess Sulis. Ever willing to adapt local customs to Roman use, they decided that Sulis was simply a variation of their own Minerva and built medicinal baths and temples on the site. The result was, in many ways, a precursor of modern Bath. The community held no administrative or military function. It existed purely for pleasure, recuperation and, for the pious, as an important religious centre. Aquae Sulis, Roman Bath, was a town of hotels, temples, shops and baths, with one great communal bathing area. It is the latter which now survives as the Roman Baths complex, one of the most impressive Roman remains in Europe. Extraordinary as these may be, it is worth remembering that they represent just part of a

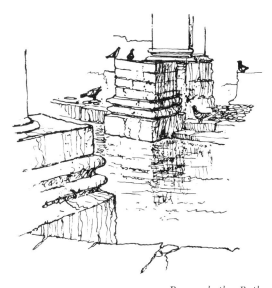

Roman baths, Bath

43

Roman settlement of some size and more social importance.

While the Romans ruled Britain, Bath flourished. After the fall of the empire, and the coming of the Dark Ages, the town fell into decay. The old gods were displaced by new ones, and finally one supreme deity. The social cohesion of the empire disappeared and the rivalry of factional infighting took its place. On a more prosaic level, the use of public baths as a social gathering place disappeared, probably overnight. Except for medicinal purposes, the people of Britain stopped bathing around the sixth century AD and remained timid of the bath for a good millennium. It was only the therapeutic properties of the spa waters which tempted them back into the tub.

But the town was not still between the disappearance of the Romans and the arrival of the Georgians. In 757 the Saxon king Offa founded a Benedictine monastery here dedicated to St Peter and the religious community grew in size and importance. In 973 Edgar was crowned King of England in Bath in the presence of the archbishops of York and Canterbury. After the Normans arrived work began on the creation of a new Abbey and a centre of monastic power. The rivalry between Bath and Wells (17 miles south west) was intense, culminating in the formation of the Bishopric of Bath *and* Wells to end the squabbling about which was greater. There was a brief reliance on the Cotswold wool trade for prosperity but the one, perennial, source of income was the mineral baths. By the early 17th century, more and more sick and infirm people were visiting Bath in the hope of a miracle cure from the hot springs, and the local authority began to view tourism as an industry to be encouraged.

Several members of the Royal family visited the city, bringing court followers and the fashionable in their wake. But the creation of the Bath we recognise today is largely due to the vision of two men: Richard 'Beau' Nash and John Wood the Elder. Nash was a man about town who virtually installed himself as Master of Ceremonies of the Bath social circle from the beginning to the middle of the 18th century. The set of codes and activities which created the social life of the city was Nash's invention. He brought music into the Pump Room and acted like the MC at a debutante's ball when it came to handing out introductions to parties and weeding out undesirables. At the height of his powers – popularity would be too strong a word – Nash could make or break any visitor to Bath, almost regardless of rank. His legacy was a city renowned for its wit, gentility and the quality of its visitors. Those at the pinnacle of European society flocked to take the waters in much the same way that today they head for Gstaad. It was a club of absolute exclusivity, attracting nobles, *nouveaux riches* and a fair smattering of authors, such as Fielding, Sheridan and Jane Austen who found ample source material for their works in the round of social gatherings which made up the average Bath day.

John Wood the Elder was the architect whose style dominates the whole city. Wood designed the country house of the Bath stone merchant, Ralph Allen, Prior Park at Combe Down. Prior Park was created as a massive advertisement both for Bath stone and Wood's architectural skills. The two went on to offer a vision of a new Bath, a city composed of tasteful homes in Bath stone – from Allen's quarries – all conforming to Wood's strict Palladian style of elegant simplicity. The clamour for new homes for the rich visitors was unstoppable and Wood's vision turned into reality. When he died, his son, John Wood the Younger, and a generation of architects continued the work to create the imposing Georgian city of today.

The heady whirl of Bath brilliance lasted no more than a few decades. The fashion for hot springs gave way to the seaside when George III decided that Weymouth and Brighton were preferable to the crowded streets and social gatherings of Bath. By the turn of the century, Bath was in decline and Victorian times saw the city turn to industry and the railway in a half-hearted attempt to restore its fortunes. It was only after the Second World War – during which parts of Bath were bombed – that tourists began to return to the city in substantial numbers. Today it is one of the major destinations in Britain and a particular favourite with American visitors. Tourism is by far the largest industry, boosted by the annual Bath Festival in late May and early June during which it is extremely difficult to find rooms in any of the major hotels.

Modern Bath is a city which entrances visitors of all generations, but it is not without its problems. The centre has difficulty coping with the traffic imposed upon it and the pedestrianised streets are almost always crowded during fine weather, sometimes unbearably so on summer weekends. To see the city properly requires some tiring walking; the Royal Crescent, an essential sight, is best seen by car for those who cannot manage steep hills. And, finally, it must be said that Ralph Allen's porous Bath stone, while perhaps admirable for the 18th century, is not the most ideal building material for the 20th century. Several parts of the city display the grimy evidence of pollution stains though there is a concerted attempt by a caring local authority to ensure that Bath presents a clean face to the world on almost every occasion, and the maintenance of Wood's creations is not for the faint-hearted. Bath is an exceptional place even if it sometimes seems that, tourists apart, it is solely populated by estate agents, 'resting' actors, waiters and damp proofing consultants.

There is a great deal to see here, almost too much. Museums flourish everywhere, even to the extent of an American museum, run by two expatriate Bath-loving Americans, which is a recreation of, well, American history and life. Add to this museums dedicated to bookbinding, fashion, the astronomer William Herschel, English naive art... the list goes on forever. Trying to tick off the items on it in a single day can become indigestible. Better to concentrate on the principal sights and nibble away at the minor ones another time.

No visit to Bath should begin anywhere but at the Roman Baths Museum. While there has been a little creative archeology in its presentation, the Baths remain an extraordinary relic of Roman Britain not just for their extent but also for their sense of continuity with ancient life in the city. It is easy to imagine the comings and goings of a pleasure-seeking Roman community here, even when the place is crowded with camera-clicking fellow tourists. There are fine mosaics and stone artefacts from the Roman period and a collection of finds from the Bath area. The recently excavated site of the temple to Sulis Minerva can now be seen with its sacrificial altar and the gilt bronze head of the goddess. Above the Baths is the Georgian Pump Room, the busy centre of Bath in the days of its social peak and still a genteel place for morning coffee or afternoon tea to the strains of the traditional Pump Room trio. You can try a glass of the spring mineral water here; it conforms to the old rule that the things which do you most good are the ones which taste most foul. Perrier has nothing to fear.

Across from the Baths is the Abbey. The Norman church was mysteriously rebuilt in the 15th century after the incumbent bishop was inspired by a dream. More prosaic reasons to do with clerical rivalry may also have played their part. The Abbey is in the Perpendicular style and by no means as impressive as its rival at Wells. There are interesting memorials to famous Bath residents, Beau Nash among them, and regular concerts. The Theatre Royal is a late Georgian theatre now fully restored and in magnificent fettle. It was familiar to most of the famous Georgian actors and now regularly serves as a proving ground for productions destined, or not, for London's West End.

Another of the city's curiosities is Pulteney Bridge, the two storey structure which spans the Avon at Bridge Street, above the weir on the river. Built in the late 18th century to a John Nash design, the bridge is unique for the period in that it revives the medieval tradition of building shops on the bridge itself, just as once happened with the main bridges of London.

John Wood's Bath lies on the hill overlooking the city, a district of large, handsome stone houses and broad, open streets. Above George Street is classical Bath, composed of fine, imposing terraced mansions, most of them in a good state of repair. The Upper Assembly Rooms here were the scene of the Georgian city's many balls and social events. To their west is the Circus, one of the elder John Wood's most acclaimed creations, a circle of Palladian mansions richly decorated with fanciful motifs all surrounding a park. Brock Street, going west from the Circus, leads to Bath's most famous address, the Royal Crescent, 30 great mansions formed in a semicircle which looks down upon the city. The first house has been restored to near its original condition and is now open as a museum. The Royal Crescent was built between 1767 and 1774 by John Wood's son and became the model for many similar crescents throughout Britain for the next half century. It overlooks the eastern end of the 57-acre Royal Victoria Park, with a seven-acre botanical garden, a boating pool and children's play area. There are several pleasant footpaths leading west and one may also walk down to the banks of the Avon, following a path back into the city through Green Park.

Bath is well furnished with open spaces. Alexandra Park, a hearty walk at the top of Beechen Cliff to the south, has superb views over the whole of the city. The central Parade Gardens, by the Avon, has brass bands and other entertainments at regular intervals. There is a maze in Beazer Gardens near Pulteney Weir to the east, and a scented garden for the blind in nearby Henrietta Park. The city's oldest park is Sydney Gardens, laid out in 1795, with Chinese bridges over the Kennet and Avon Canal.

This is a city to be explored on foot, and many more surprises lie waiting in its streets than can be listed here. Parking facilities are overstretched and unreliable – the best bet with Bath is to find a hotel a little way from town, leave your vehicle there and set out in exploration with a good pair of shoes and an enquiring mind. Few will return disappointed.

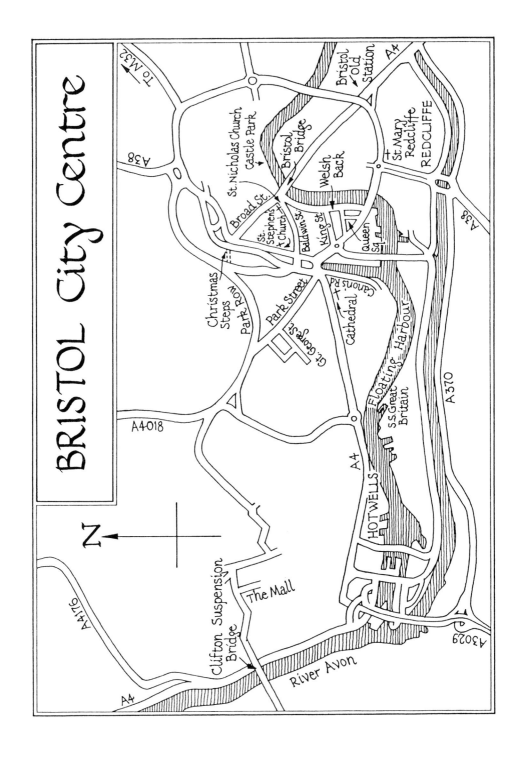

BRISTOL City Centre

Bristol

For all its size – the population of more than 400,000 makes the city the largest in the West Country – Bristol is a place of great interest and considerable appeal. The city is less dependent on the tourist for its income than Bath and has a much more varied history. While, inevitably, areas have given way to redevelopment and the demands of modern industry, Bristol retains an individual character closely allied to its historic past. It is a city likely to convert those with an apathy for urban life; here the visitor can wander around picturesque medieval streets, take tea by the renovated docks, and walk through the pleasant parkland of Clifton, all in the same day.

The sea is, of course, the most important influence to affect the development of Bristol over the centuries, since its foundation as a small shipping town under the Saxons. The city lies close to the Bristol Channel with a natural defence for shipping. When Britain became a maritime nation, Bristol prospered, growing at an astonishing rate until, in the 14th century, it was the most prosperous provincial town in the country. Bristol mariners were in the forefront of every development of the nation's sea trade, making links along the Mediterranean and to Iceland by the 15th century. When Europe began to look west for new trade routes, Bristol responded. In 1497, five years after Columbus had discovered the 'New World', John Cabot set sail from Bristol and charted the North American mainland for the first time.

For the next three centuries, maritime shipping was to bring great wealth to the city, and help it forge strong business and family links with America. The states of the New World were supplied with slaves, skills and money from Bristol ships which returned to the Old World with tobacco, rum and other new products in their holds. It was a golden age in the city's fortunes. Rich merchants built delightful small churches on the proceeds of the trade explosion, grand mansions appeared and with it a bustling dockside community of sea captains and more humble mariners looking for work. The name of Bristol was known to sailors throughout the world and found its way into literature. The Admiral Benbow inn in Stevenson's *Treasure Island* is reputed to be based on the 17th-century Llandoger Trow pub, still pulling pints in ancient King Street, and Daniel Defoe used the same inn for his interviews with the castaway Alexander Selkirk who was to prove the model for *Robinson Crusoe*.

Like many maritime cities of its kind, Bristol began to feel the cold wind of competition by the end of the 18th century. The newly independent American states looked elsewhere for European partners and other transatlantic ports, notably Liverpool, began to attract away traditional Bristol trade.

Victorian Bristol was dominated by the figure of Isambard Kingdom Brunel, the engineer. He proposed the idea of a new, faster link between London and America, along his Great Western Railway to Bristol, then into his *Great Britain* steamship. The *Great Britain* was never one of Brunel's major successes although it was the first iron ship every built and a pioneer of the screw propeller. But the Great Western Railway was, for many years, one of the most famous lines in Britain though it is now submerged in the British Rail network. Brunel's other great creation in Bristol is the Clifton Suspension Bridge, a distinctive image of the city which spans the Avon Gorge in the attractive suburb to the west of the city.

Modern Bristol is an affluent place of many facets. The docks continue to work on international trade, but the city has also maintained its engineering and manufacturing interests, while expanding into high technology. At the end of the M4 corridor, its many social attractions have made it a popular place for siting new companies, and the ease of travel to London along the fast Paddington line of Brunel's original Great

Clifton Bridge

Western has persuaded many city commuters to make their home alongside the Avon.

Central Bristol is easily explored on foot. Clifton, set on a hill, is best reached by car. Ferries regularly leave several points along the Floating Harbour to reach the older parts of the dock. The easiest ferry point for the new visitor to find is the one close to the Watershed Media Centre.

There is an obvious landmark for beginning any tour of Bristol. It is the statue of Neptune which stands by the waterside overlooking the area called The Centre, the small green at the heart of the old city. Looking back towards modern Bristol one could be forgiven for thinking that little of the old city remains, but this is mistaken. Almost hidden by the hubbub of 20th-century Bristol, lie small, photogenic areas of immense charm. To the left, walking from Neptune, lies the Edwardian Hippodrome theatre and the old quarter around Christmas Steps, a stone thoroughfare rising steeply from river level to the hill above. At the top is the small 15th-century chapel of the Three Kings of Cologne and a group of almshouses built in a fanciful Victorian Gothic style.

To the right, behind busy Baldwin Street, can be found St Nicholas Markets, a busy and interesting market of food, antiques and bric-a-brac which has survived the supermarket age. Part of the markets complex is the original Corn Exchange of 1743 designed by John Wood the Elder, one of the creators of Bath. The four bronze pillars outside the Exchange date from the late 16th century and were used as trading tables by merchants. Their name, the Nails, gave rise to the saying 'to pay on the Nail'.

St Nicholas' Church has now been converted into a museum with a brass rubbing centre and a display of paintings, among them Hogarth's altarpiece originally produced for the church of St Mary Redcliffe. The most attractive church of the area is St Stephen's, dating from the 15th century, which has a memorial to Martin Pring who discovered Plymouth Harbour in New England where the *Mayflower* later anchored. At the end of Broad Street, home of the Grand Hotel and the Victorian Guild Hall, is St John's Church which incorporates one of the medieval entrance arches to the city.

Below Baldwin Street is the handsome Queen Square, watched over by a statue of William III on horseback. Around here lie some of the most characterful streets and houses of old Bristol. King Street remains essentially medieval, with a variety of architectural styles standing cheek by jowl in happy disorder. The Theatre Royal, dating from 1766, claims to be the oldest theatre in the country to have run continuous

Bristol Docks

performances since its opening. Now the home of the Bristol Old Vic, Kean, Garrick and Ellen Terry have appeared on its still-preserved Georgian stage. Close to the water stands the city's most historic pub, the Llandoger Trow, a timbered pile of indefinable allure which still manages to overcome the news, plastered on the front, that it is now a Berni Inn. Opposite stands the battered Old Duke, an archetypal spit and sawdust pub with a well-deserved reputation as a live jazz venue. A few yards away, moored by the quayside lane of Welsh Back, is The Lightship now converted into a pub and nightclub. These three watering holes make this little section of the city a magnet for the local nightlife, particularly in summer when visitors can eat and drink outside in the pedestrianised area. Rowing boats can be hired from Welsh Back and there is a ferry point. Bristol Bridge, to the north, lies on medieval foundations on the site of the oldest bridge into the city.

Beyond Queen Square, over the Floating Harbour, lies Redcliffe and the church of St Mary Redcliffe, memorably described by Elizabeth I as 'the fairest, goodliest and most famous parish church in England'. The centre of Bristol was badly bombed during the Second World War, and Redcliffe suffered particularly badly, though the church survived unscathed. It is a little too grand to be fairly described as a 'parish church'. Its ornateness and size owe much to a local merchant family, the Canynges, who paid for its completion during the 15th century. One of its greatest benefactors, William Canynge, was a Member of Parliament for the city who took to the priesthood. He is still remembered in a civic service every Whit Sunday during which the floor of the chancel is covered with rushes.

Bristol Old Station, by the side of the existing modern station of Temple Meads, is Brunel's original terminus for the Great Western Railway, built in 1840 it is now undergoing restoration and is due to be the home for the Exploratory, a science centre offering visitors the chance to use pieces of scientific equipment in real experiments. The building's bold construction emphasises the importance placed by its designer on the new mass transport technology of the railways. The train shed has an astonishing hammerbeam roof that echoes those of some of the region's great churches. Temple Church nearby dates from the 12th century and was virtually destroyed during the war, though the simple tower remains. The church was once the property of the Knights Templar.

South of Neptune's Statue can be found the old harbour area of St Augustine's Reach, currently undergoing redevelopment but already a considerable attraction for visitors. The Watershed is an arts centre with cinemas, restaurants and bars and also the Arnolfini, a nationally acclaimed centre for the contemporary arts. The Bristol Industrial Museum is one of the best of its kind in the country, reflecting the great industrial heritage of the city. Road and rail vehicles dating back three centuries can be seen and there is an excellent display of the city's role in aviation history with an aircraft dating from 1910 and a full-size cockpit from the partly locally built Concorde. The National Lifeboat Museum is a unique institution telling the story of the work of voluntary lifeboats over the centuries. Throughout the area there is a wide selection of engaging pubs and restaurants catering for locals and visitors alike.

The city's other interesting harbour area, Hotwells, is a long walk, an easy ferry journey, or a quick train ride on the harbour railway from the Industrial Museum. It lies to the west, on the island bounded by the Avon on one side and the Floating Harbour on the other. Here Brunel's superb SS *Great Britain* can be found, undergoing restoration in the same dock where she was built. It is a magnificent vessel, epitomising the proud vision of the Victorian era, and accompanied by a museum which tells the history of the great ship. Further west, the docks have been transformed into a leisure area for recreation, dining and evening drinkers. Canoes, small boats, and windsurfers mingle with anglers and bystanders and there is even a popular caravan site, managed by the Caravan Club of Great Britain, on the old Baltic Wharf. Few cities anywhere in the world can boast such a sociable waterside amenity.

The east of the city was devastated by German bombers but one important building remains. The New Room in Broadmead was the first Methodist chapel, opened by John Wesley in 1739. The wooden interior, with its double-decked pulpit, is particularly memorable. Bristol was a favourite city for dissenters. George Fox, the founder of the Quakers, was married in Quakers' Friars nearby, once the cloisters of a Dominican friary founded in the 13th century. Castle Park is on the site of the Norman city castle demolished by Cromwell in 1656 so that it could not be used by rebellious forces, supporters of the exiled Charles. Until the Second World War, this was a business and residential district.

The remaining city sights of Bristol lie to the west of Neptune's statue. Bristol Cathedral is a polyglot creation of several centuries, but note the attractive 16th-century Abbey Gateway to the west, the fine Norman chapter house and a set of candlesticks donated to the cathedral in 1712 by the privateers who rescued Alexander Selkirk, Defoe's inspiration for Robinson Crusoe. Brandon Hill served as a fort during the Civil War and

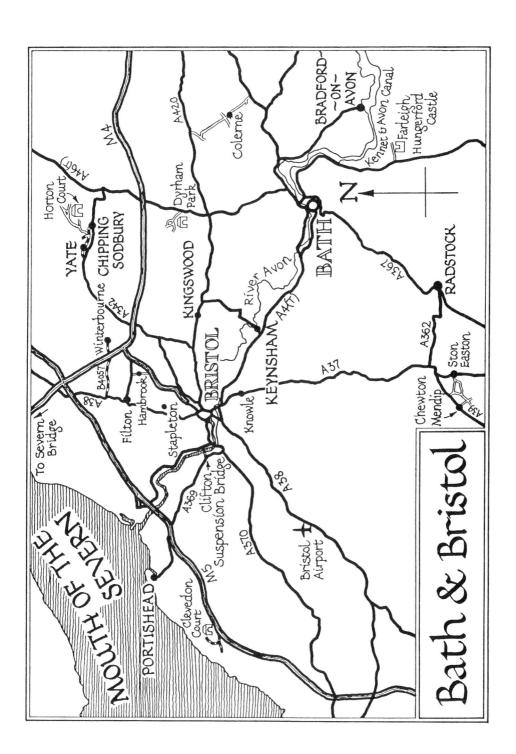

Bath & Bristol

is now topped with the Cabot tower, erected by the Victorians to mark the journey of John Cabot to the New World. There are good views of the city from the top. The City Museum and Art Gallery is richly endowed with paintings by Renoir and Delacroix and cultural collections from all over the world. The natural history collection, with live displays of local animals and freshwater fish, is exceptional.

Two local houses open to the public are of outstanding interest. The Red Lodge in Park Row is a 16th-century mansion with 18th-century additions. The interior has splendid furnishings from both periods while a replica Tudor garden is being created outside. The Georgian House, Great George Street, just off Park Street, is furnished much as it would have been when it was first occupied by a sugar merchant with interests in the West Indies and offers fascinating insights into Georgian life.

Clifton is the smart suburb which runs along the eastern side of the Avon Gorge. Brunel's Suspension Bridge is, inevitably, its chief attraction, though there is much else to see. The bridge spans 702 feet across the gorge and, at high tide, stands around 245 feet above the water. In 1885 a local woman who was jilted by her lover leapt from the bridge but survived the fall when her descent was cushioned by the ballooning petticoats popular at the time. Clifton is home to Bristol Zoo, one of Britain's most popular zoos, with 12 acres of grounds and a rich collection of animals, birds, reptiles and fish. The village is a pleasant place for a stroll, with attractive stone streets, small antique shops, and a plethora of old pubs and more modern restaurants. To the north lie the Downs, an area of park and woodlands which lead out of the city by the Avon Gorge and afford views across the Bristol Channel to Wales.

Bristol prides itself on its annual round of public events. The Powerboat Grand Prix, held each June, attracts more than 200,000 spectators for the races around the docks area. July sees an international clientele for the World Wine Fair and each August Bank Holiday is reserved for a maritime carnival. The city's regatta takes place in July while in June there is a Festival of the Sea, celebrating the maritime past with exhibitions and films and a sea shanty festival. In August there is a spectacular hot air balloon festival in Ashton Court Estate which can attract more than 250,000 visitors; in the same month there is also the annual city flower show. Christmas illuminations appear on the city streets six weeks before the holiday, and the weekend before Christmas is the time for a water carnival with carol singing by the harbour. The Tourist Information Centre can advise on precise dates for these events: do book your accommodation in advance.

Tourist Information

Abbey Church Yard
Bath
Tel: 0225 462831

14 Narrow Quay
Bristol
Tel: 0272 260767

Hotels

Royal Crescent Hotel
16 Royal Crescent
5m S Bath
Avon
Tel: 0225 339401
Luxurious first class hotel in the famous
town houses of the Crescent form Bath's
most sought-after address. Part of the
Norfolk Capital group.
Rooms: 45
Credit cards: Access, Visa, Amex, Diners
Rating *****

Ston Easton Park
Chewton Mendip
Avon
Tel: 076121 631
Palladian mansion converted into
luxurious hotel with award-winning
restaurant.
Rooms: 20
Credit cards: Access, Visa, Amex, Diners
Rating *****

Homewood Park
Hinton Charterhouse
5m S Bath
Avon
Tel: 022122 3731
Beautiful country hotel with good
restaurant in 10 acres of gardens.
Rooms: 15
Credit cards: Access, Visa, Amex, Diners
Rating *****

The Priory
Weston Road
Bath
Tel: 0225 331922
Elegant Georgian house in its own two
acres some way from town. Slightly less
expensive than the Royal Crescent.
Rooms: 21
Credit cards: Access, Visa, Amex, Diners
Rating *****

Somerset House
35 Bathwick Hill
Bath
Avon
Tel: 0225 66451/63471
No smoking hotel with good restaurant
and views of the city.
Rooms: 9
Credit cards: Access, Visa, Amex
Rating **

Old Malt House Hotel
Radford Timsbury
Bath
Tel: 0761 70106
Characterful country house hotel.
Rooms: 10
Credit cards: Access, Visa, Amex, Diners
Rating ***

Grand Hotel
Broad Street
Bristol
Tel: 0272 291645
The city's traditional town centre hotel
well-placed for all sights and amenities.
Rooms: 179
Credit cards: Access, Visa, Amex, Diners
Rating *****

Private Accommodation

Burnett Manor
Keynsham
Avon
Tel: 0272 863600

Burnett Manor contd
Medieval manor five miles from Bath
and Bristol.
Rooms: 2
Credit cards: none
Rating **

Merfield House
Rode
Bath
Tel: 0373 830298
Georgian house 10 miles from Bath.
Rooms: 3
Credit cards: none
Rating **

2 Cove House
Ashton Keynes
Wilts
Tel: 0285 861221
Part of a 17th-century manor house six
miles south of Cirencester.
Rooms: 3
Credit cards: none
Rating ***

Parsonage Farmhouse
High Street
Colerne
Wilts
Tel: 0225 742811
Attractive farmhouse off the A420 Bristol
to Chippenham road.
Rooms: 2
Credit cards: none
Rating **

Chilvester Hill House
Calne
Wilts
Tel: 0249 813981/815785
Victorian house in seven acres.
Rooms: 3
Credit cards: Access, Visa, Amex, Diners
Rating ***

Priory Steps
Newtown
Bradford-on-Avon
Wilts
Tel: 02216 2230
Former weavers' cottages close to town
centre only eight miles from Bath.
Rooms: 5
Credit cards: Access, Visa
Rating ***

Restaurants

Dower House
Royal Crescent Hotel
Royal Crescent
Bath
Tel: 0225 319090
Ex-Ritz chef Michael Croft offers superb
food in fine surroundings. Fish, shellfish
and game according to the markets.
Booking essential at weekends and busy
periods.
Credit cards: Access, Visa, Amex, Diners
Rating *****

Circus Restaurant
34 Brock Street
Bath
Tel: 0225 330208
Imaginative French and English food in
the Georgian old town.
Credit cards: Access, Visa, Amex
Rating ****

Beaujolais
5 Chapel Row
Bath
Tel: 0225 23417
Traditional French food in old house
with tables outside in summer. Closed
Sundays.
Credit cards: Access, Visa
Rating ***

Cafe des Amis du Vin
10 The Mall
Clifton
Bristol
Tel: 0272 741386
Traditional French food in one of
Clifton's many good restaurants.
Credit cards: Access, Visa, Amex, Diners
Rating ***

China Palace
18a Baldwin Street
Bristol
Tel: 0272 262719
Authentic and interesting Cantonese food
in city centre.
Credit cards: Access, Visa, Amex, Diners
Rating ***

Watershed Media Centre
1 Canons Road
Bristol
Tel: 0272 214135
Inexpensive English and continental food
in the Watershed's busy brasserie.
Credit cards: Access, Visa
Rating **

Historic Houses

Clevedon Court (NT)
Clevedon
Medieval manor house with pottery and
glass on show. March to September 2.30-
5, Sundays, Wednesdays and Thursdays.

Dyrham Park (NT)
Abson
8m N Bath
Magnificent 17th-century mansion
virtually unchanged since it was built.
Grounds of 263 acres with fallow deer.
Park open all year 12-5.30; house March
to October 2-5.30, closed Thursdays and
Fridays.

Horton Court (NT)
3m NE Chipping Sodbury
Norman hall from the 12th century and a
Perpendicular ambulatory. March to
October, 2-5.30 Wednesdays and
Saturdays.

Ancient Monuments

Farleigh Hungerford Castle
Farleigh Hungerford
3m W Trowbridge
Ruined 14th-century castle once the
home of the notorious Hungerfords,
variously executed for murder, treason
and adultery. Well preserved family
chapel. Summer 10-6 daily; winter 10-4,
closed Mondays.

Museums

Roman Baths Museum and
Temple Precinct
Stall Street
Bath
The city's most famous sight, the original
main Roman bath with a rich Roman
museum. Winter weekdays 9-5, Sundays
10-7. March to October, weekdays and
Sundays 9-6; July to August weekdays
and Sundays 9-7.

1 Royal Crescent
Royal Crescent
Bath
The first house in the famous crescent
now converted into a period museum
with contemporary furniture and
decorations. March to Christmas
Tuesday to Saturday 11-5; Sunday 2-5.

Museum of English Naive Art
Old Schoolroom
The Vineyards
The Paragon
Bath

Museum of English Naive Art contd
English folk painting of the 18th and 19th
centuries. April to October daily 11-6,
Sundays 2-6.

Geology Museum
18 Queen Square
Bath
Display of varied local geology. Monday
to Friday 9.30-6, Saturdays 9.30-5.

The American Museum in Britain
Claverton Down
Bath
A fine 1820 manor house which now
contains historical collections of
American furnishings and a replica of
part of Washington's garden at Mount
Vernon. March to October daily 2-5,
closed Mondays.

Museum of Bookbinding
Manvers Street
Bath
Displays of bookbinding techniques
through the ages. Weekdays 9-5.

Herschel House and Museum
19 New King Street
Bath
Home of polymath William Herschel
who discovered the planet Uranus while
working here in 1781. March to October
daily 2-5, winter Sundays only.

Sally Lunn's Kitchen Museum
Bath
The oldest house in the city, between
Abbey Green and the Fernley Hotel, with
original kitchen equipment. Mornings
only 10-1, closed Sundays.

Bath Postal Museum
8 Broad Street
Bath
Philatelist's heaven with reproduction
Victorian Post Office. Monday to
Saturday 11-5.

Bath Industrial Heritage Centre
Julian Road
Bath
Reconstruction of Victorian factory
providing displays of stoneworking and
cabinet makers' workshop. February to
November daily 2-5, December and
January weekends only 2-5.

The Exploratory
Bristol Old Station
Bristol
Science centre with practical displays of
inventions and scientific principles – great
fun for children and adults alike. Daily
except Christmas holiday 10-5.

Walks

Free guided tours of Bath led by
volunteers leave from outside the Pump
Room. From May to October they take
place at 10.30am Mondays and
Thursdays, 10.30am and 2.30pm
Wednesdays and Sundays, 10.30am and
7pm Tuesdays and Fridays and 7pm
Saturdays. In winter they take place at
10.30am daily except Sundays when there
is an additional tour at 2.30pm.

Dorchester High Street

3 The Dorset Coast

From the unique coastal town of Lyme Regis to the beautiful modern resort of Poole, the Dorset coast offers lovely countryside, good walks and historic connections. The coast is linked by a designated footpath. A visit to this area can easily be combined with inland Dorset (see pp. 82-95) or tied in with a visit to neighbouring East Devon. The amount of time needed for a trip here depends on how active the visitor wishes to be. There is much splendid walking to be had, and a trip to Brownsea Island alone can take up at least half a day. But it is also possible to tick off the principal sights by car in three days. A leisurely visit to the entire area would best be organised by dividing time between two bases, one in the east and one in the west. Poole, Swanage and Lyme Regis are all attractive established places to stay, with good facilities, but there are many small village pubs and bed and breakfast establishments along the length of the coast. Weymouth is a large and busy beach resort with little individual character.

Lyme Regis

The popular novel and film of *The French Lieutenant's Woman*, by the local writer John Fowles, brought the curious little seaside town of Lyme Regis to the world's attention. Situated at the far west of the county, close to the Devon border, Lyme has been popular with visitors for centuries – it was Jane Austen's favourite coastal resort and Daniel Defoe was another admirer – and has been little spoilt by the 20th century in spite of the summer crowds.

There is no coastal resort quite like Lyme; it is not, in a conventional sense, particularly beautiful, though there are several fine houses, mainly Georgian, to be found in the older streets. The beach is rocky and the geology of the surrounding land unstable, leading to cliff falls which can endanger the careless walker. The town's charm lies in its unusual location and the distinctive local coastline, with the attractive little harbour of the Cobb and the nearby Undercliff, splendid walking country, rich in birds and flowers. The town of Lyme lies in an odd location, set on the steep sides of the ravine leading to the ancient harbour. Since most hotels lie a little way from the centre of the town, and it is difficult to park close to the centre, this can make for some strenuous walking.

Lyme is one of the oldest ports in the region, partly thanks to the breakwater of the Cobb which was built in the 14th century. The name 'Regis' stems from a royal charter first awarded in 1284. Lyme mariners were stalwart supporters of the English kings, fighting in virtually every major sea battle including the Armada in which five Lyme ships harried the mighty fleet of Spain. It was here that the Duke of Monmouth landed in 1685, intent on dislodging the Catholic James II from the throne and installing himself as a Protestant monarch. His cause received a surprising level of support in Lyme; the town had suffered a two-month siege by Royalists during the Civil War only 40 years earlier and might have been expected to have fought shy of any exploit which could lead it into conflict again so soon. After Monmouth's defeat at Sedgmoor and subsequent execution, 12 Lyme men were hanged on the town beach as a warning to future rebels.

All the principal pleasures of Lyme are connected with the sea. From the town centre, with its pleasant and occasionally colourful Georgian façades, runs a plain seafront esplanade which leads to the Cobb, a magnet for walkers from miles around. Yachtsmen, bathers and fishermen co-exist happily on the ancient breakwater and there is a profusion of little cafés and pubs catering for the holiday trade. The crumbling cliffs of the area are a rich source of well-preserved fossils; some of the best examples found in Britain have been discovered in the cliffs around Lyme. The dinosaur connection is celebrated in

Lyme Regis, Dorset

'Dinosaurland', an exhibition of fossils and models of dinosaurs in a listed building close to the town centre.

There are excellent walks to both sides of the town, though care should be taken to avoid subsidence and the longer excursions are not for the faint-hearted. Each August the town celebrates with a modest regatta and carnival – book rooms in advance to be certain of accommodation.

Abbotsbury

The main road from Lyme eastward runs inland. Follow it until Bridport where a minor coastal road to Weymouth branches to the right. Bridport and West Bay form the largest town in west Dorset, though that means only a mere 6,800 residents. It is a functional town which, since medieval times, has been one of the principal rope-making centres in Britain. West Bay was known as Bridport Harbour until it was renamed by the Great Western Railway Company which had plans to turn it into a popular resort to rival Weymouth or Bournemouth. The masses never came; today West Bay is a modest resort of little character, but there are good beaches and walks along the Dorset Coastal Path.

The village of Abbotsbury makes a spectacular appearance on the road to Weymouth. Outside the village, on a lonely hill, stands the atmospheric St Catherine's Chapel, as moody an ancient monument as Glastonbury's Tor. With a fine village hotel, the Ilchester Arms, Abbotsbury is an excellent place to stay for anyone who wishes to avoid the tourist bustle of the larger towns.

Two miles north west of the village, Abbotsbury Castle is an Iron Age hillfort some 700 feet above sea level, with walks over its ten acres and, on a clear day, good views over the Channel. The development of the village stems from the once important Benedictine Abbey – its name means abbot's manor. The gatehouse and huge tithe barn of the 11th-century abbey remain. The village church of St Nicholas is 15th century with some earlier features. Bullet holes in the pulpit are said to have been caused during a skirmish between Royalist and Parliamentary forces during the Civil War, though this may be fanciful.

Abbotsbury is a quiet village of considerable charm, good for local walks and visits to neighbouring towns. A stroll to St Catherine's Chapel is pretty much essential if the weather is fine; the exposed hill can be something of a strain when the wind is whipping rain straight off the

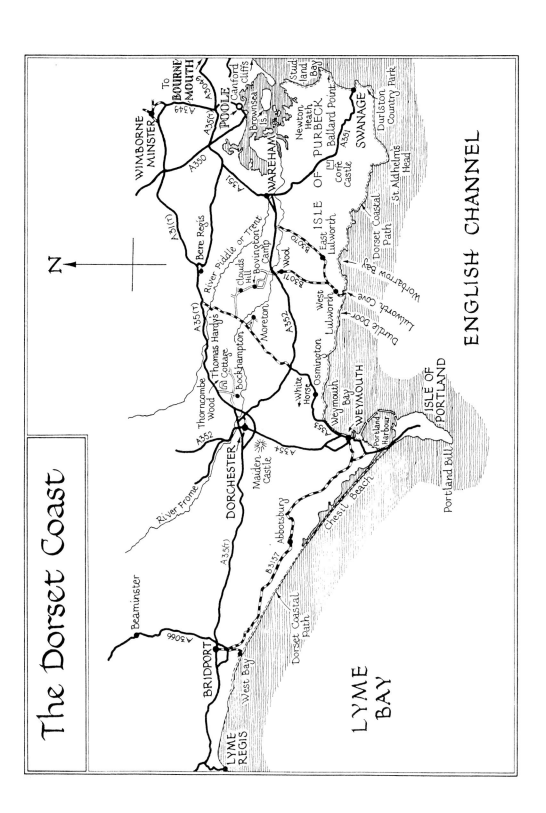

The Dorset Coast

sea. Abbotsbury is equally renowned for its swannery, a colony of mute swans founded by the abbey originally for food. The colony lives on the waters of the Fleet behind Chesil Beach, a sandbank much loved by sea fishermen which runs from Bridport to Portland.

Dorchester

To Hardy lovers, Dorchester will always be the Casterbridge of the great author's Wessex tales. This is the county town of Dorset, but a small and modest little place all the same. Hardy would be at home in most of modern Dorchester though, as a trained architect, he would certainly cast a disapproving eye at some of the characterless modern development which has taken place. Nevertheless, Dorchester is an essential stop for any visitor to southern Dorset, for its history, its beauty and the pleasant walks in the neighbourhood.

This is an historic part of England. South west of the town is one of the great ancient fortresses of the country, Maiden Castle, a vast hillfort which deserves a visit. Only from its bleak ramparts, with views for many miles over the surrounding countryside, can one appreciate the scale of what was one of the region's principal fortified encampments. Maiden Castle dates back to the Late Stone Age. By the time of the Roman invasion, it was a fortified town, defended by multiple ramparts and ditches and sling-throwing soldiers. These measures were effective against the town's traditional enemies but useless against the might of the organised and practised regiments of the Roman empire. A precise account of the fall of Maiden Castle has been assembled by historians. Shortly after the Roman landing in AD 44, the fortress was attacked by the 2nd Augusta Legion under the command of Vespasian. The Romans selected the weaker eastern gate for their assault, first launching bolts then following with infantry. There was a bloody battle in which a large part of the castle's inhabitants died before the Romans withdrew, leaving the now subdued town.

Excavations have uncovered firm evidence of the fighting and in the county museum in Dorchester visitors can see the skeleton of an unfortunate Briton with a Roman bolt embedded in his spine. The dead were usually buried where they fell, but with some elements of pagan ritual, such as interring items of food and drink with them. Apart from a brief period during the Dark Ages when there was a temple on the hill, the site has not been occupied since the Romans stormed it.

Vespasian's forces laid the foundation stones for the creation of a new Roman town on the site of modern Dorchester, Durnovaria. Many Roman finds have been unearthed in the area, as the county museum testifies. A smaller Neolithic henge, Maumbury Rings a short walk just outside the old Roman boundary of the town, was later developed by the Romans to become an amphitheatre. Their bloody sports found an echo in a later age; the Rings were used for public executions during the 18th century.

Modern Dorchester is largely Georgian and Victorian. The Antelope Hotel is earlier, and in 1685 was used by Judge Jeffreys as a makeshift court for the Bloody Assize, the trial of Monmouth's supporters during the rebellion of that year. The infamous judge tried 340 prisoners and sent 74 of them to the terrible death reserved for treason, to be hanged until nearly dead, drawn and quartered. Many others were transported as slaves to the West Indies. Close to the Antelope is the old courthouse of the Shire Hall where six more famous victims heard sentence passed upon them. It was here that the Tolpuddle Martyrs were sentenced to transportation for forming an illegal trade union in 1834, an event still marked by the British labour movement as a watershed in its history.

The county museum is a first class establishment, twice winner of the Museum of the Year award, and would do credit to any major English city. Hardy's study in his Dorchester home has been reassembled precisely as it was on the day he died and there are interesting displays on local history, archeology and geology. The keep of the Dorset Regiment now houses the Dorset Military Museum with its long record of the military exploits of the region's soldiers. The town's third museum in Icen Way is devoted to dinosaurs, the remains of which are frequently found in Dorset's soft rock. There are surviving sections of Roman wall and, behind the County Hall, the foundations of an excavated Roman town house.

Thomas Hardy is Dorset's best known resident but two other sons of the town deserve mention. A bronze in High Street West recalls the folk poet William Barnes (1801-1885) who wrote in the county dialect and was immensely popular in his day (see p. 89). Sir Frederick Treves (1853-1923), a friend of Hardy, was a Royal surgeon now best known for his discovery of the 'Elephant Man', the unfortunate Joseph Merrick. Treves was born at 8 Cornhill, opposite the Antelope Hotel, and also wrote a charming travel book on his home county, *Highways and Byways of Dorset* (1906).

Weymouth Harbour

The cottage where Hardy was born at Bockhampton is an obvious excursion from the town. There is also an interesting nature trail from the town along the banks of the Mill Stream which feeds the Frome, the county's second longest river. Take the path from the White Hart Inn on the far side of the river past the caravan site. This follows the river, past Hangman's Cottage, once the home of the town's executioner, to the footbridge known as the Blue Bridge where the trail ends. There is a wealth of plants, flowers and birds along the length of the stream; heron, kingfishers and swifts are regular visitors. From Dorchester the visitor can follow an agreeable itinerary along the Dorset coast or head inland, through Cerne Abbas with its famous hillside giant, to the towns and villages of north Dorset, see pp. 82-95.

Weymouth and Portland

Directly south of Dorchester lies the resort town of Weymouth and the curiosity of the Isle of Portland. Neither is as obviously attractive as the less developed parts of Dorset and the visitor in a hurry may feel that they could be skipped in favour of continuing east, along the beautiful coastline leading to Swanage. The leisurely traveller will find some interest here, however.

Weymouth is one of Britain's oldest seaside resorts. An important port since the 10th century, its fortunes were transformed in the early 19th century when it became a favourite watering place for George III. The king's octagonal bathing machine, set on vast cartwheels, is preserved in the town museum. The bay is superb, with excellent beaches and a wide range of watersports from windsurfing to waterskiing. The central old town is comprised of long, narrow streets of largely Georgian houses, and there are buildings of a similar age around the busy harbour which is now used by ferries to the Channel Islands and Cherbourg. Day trips to the French port are available at very low prices.

Modern Weymouth is the epitome of the family seaside resort and has withstood the pressures on its type over the past few decades remarkably well. There are seaside shows in the Pavilion on the Esplanade, Punch and Judy on the beach and the mechanical chatter of amusement arcades everywhere. Nevertheless, some other items of interest remain on the seafront. The gilded statue of George III was erected in 1810 to mark the 50th year of his reign. The Gloucester Hotel, a little further along the Esplanade, was built by the king's brother, the

Duke of Gloucester, who first introduced the king to the town. George III was, of course, eccentric to say the very least. Contemporary records say that his preferred method of bathing was to climb into the octagonal chamber, be pulled into the water by shire horses, then stand in the water nude while a small chamber orchestra played in the background.

The Jubilee clock on the Esplanade, erected in 1887 to commemorate Queen Victoria's Jubilee, is a red and blue piece of civic regalia reminiscent of past Weymouth. At the end of the Esplanade is the Lodmoor Country Park, a leisure enterprise which, at the time of writing, includes an interesting sealife centre, a butterfly farm, tropical bird park and shire horse farm. Behind the town centre is Radipole Lake, home to the town's swannery, a nature reserve run by the RSPB but of distinctly less attraction than that of Abbotsbury. Nothe Fort, now open to visitors, is a Victorian fort built on a small peninsula to protect both Weymouth and Portland harbours. There is a collection of military hardware and pleasant gardens.

Portland, Hardy's 'Isle of Slingers', is a real curiosity, a military island now connected to the mainland by a narrow road, which sweeps to the southern tip of Portland Bill, a name familiar for its use as a weather station. Bleak is an inadequate word for Portland. There is scarcely a tree in the place, and its use as an active naval base does nothing to improve first impressions. Yet this is a historic part of Dorset. Portland stone, favoured by great sculptors and the architect Sir Christopher Wren who used it for St Paul's Cathedral, was quarried here for centuries. The rocky outcrop was developed as a naval base by Henry VIII who built the Castle, now open to the public though inside the modern naval base. Convict labour took 50 years to build the enormous breakwater of Portland Harbour, a crucial mustering point for craft involved in the D-Day landings. There is a small museum devoted to island life and a desolate, eerie drive to the Bill itself. The arid atmosphere of Portland is unique and memorable if not, in the slightest sense, beautiful.

Lulworth

The heritage coastline between Weymouth and Poole must count as some of the finest in the country. The Dorset Coastal Path runs the length of the coast, past the bays of Weymouth, Ringstead, Lulworth Cove and Worbarrow Bay to St Aldhelm's Head. There are only inland roads in this part of the county; for the most part the coastline is utterly unspoilt and quite delightful for walkers.

Leave Weymouth by the main A353 trunk road to Poole. The giant figure on a white horse cut into the chalk after Osmington is another Weymouth paean to George III in thanks for his role in popularising the town. Before Wool, turn right onto the minor road signposted to Lulworth, one of Dorset's most acclaimed beauty spots. The place is divided in two – West and East Lulworth, and, in essence, is a tiny seaside resort set in the gorgeous location of Lulworth Cove, a precise circular bay of undamaged charm. The coastline hereabouts represents a classic case of erosion, straight out of a school textbook. The chalk downlands support a fascinating array of wild creatures and one unique local butterfly, the Lulworth Skipper.

Small boats go fishing from the tiny landing of the cove and sell their catch to first comers or take visitors for boat rides. There is more money to be made from fishing for tourists than for mackerel; in the summer the pressure on the limited and outrageously expensive car park facilities can be overwhelming. Plan to arrive early if you want to walk in the gorgeous surrounding countryside along the line of the coastal path. The cliffs rise to 400 feet and are rich in fossils. To the west, Durdle Door, a great rock arch carved by the sea over the centuries, is another natural feature which rivals Lulworth Cove for the visitor's attention. Take note of the local signs which indicate whether firing is taking place on the local army ranges; occasionally walkers are barred from parts of the area for their own safety.

Both Lulworth villages are attractive though occasionally overrun. There is a small 12th-century chapel, founded by a Cistercian abbey, near the cove and, in East Lulworth, an 18th-century castle currently closed to the public.

Leave Lulworth by the B3070 to the west, through wild heathland much used by the army for firing ranges and tank training. Wareham, back on the main A352, is a busy, pleasant market town of Saxon origins. A lifesize effigy of T. E. Lawrence, 'Lawrence of Arabia', dressed in the robes of the Middle East, stands in the Saxon St Martins Church marking the area's links with this unhappy, itinerant explorer. Lawrence, after his famous exploits in the Middle East, settled at Clouds Hill near Bere Regis. He died after a mysterious motorcycle accident nearby in 1935. The house is now open to visitors and his grave is close by at Moreton. The siting of the statue in Wareham carries an odd tale. The effigy was originally made for Salisbury cathedral but it was refused because of

71

Lawrence's lifestyle – he was a homosexual. Wareham accepted it instead; few would think that this was anything but Salisbury's loss.

The road south from Wareham to Swanage leads to Corfe Castle, a village with a ruined fortress which must count as one of the most photographed monuments in Wessex. Corfe is a perpetually handsome place in grey stone dominated by the snag-toothed castle ruins above it. The castle at Corfe was an important fortress in the area for centuries. Legend has it that it was here, in 978, that the young King Edward, later known as the martyr, was murdered. During the Civil War, it was then under the ownership of the Attorney General, Sir John Banks, who supported the Royalist cause and went to fight with the king, leaving his wife to defend the castle. She and her supporters endured two harsh sieges by the Parliamentary forces until, in 1646, she was tricked into defeat when one of the garrison officers betrayed the cause and allowed the Parliamentary forces into the castle. Cromwell ordered that the great castle be slighted – reduced to ruins – as a punishment to the family and it has stood in ruins to this day. There is a fine village church with obscure, fantastic gargoyles.

Swanage and the Isle of Purbeck

Poole and Swanage would doubtless vie, in the minds of most independent visitors, for the title of Wessex's finest seaside resort. For the lover of open countryside and an Edwardian air, Swanage will certainly win the prize. It is difficult to pin down this little resort's innate charm which manages to embrace the family atmosphere of Weymouth and Bournemouth without the unfortunate tat and glitter. The attractiveness of Swanage probably depends as much on what has not happened to the town as what has.

The resort lies in its own bay at the eastern end of the Purbeck peninsula, the Isle of Purbeck. Behind it is the open countryside of the Durlston Country Park, superb walking countryside of 261 acres well managed by the county council. Swanage is a timeless place which makes an excellent base for exploring all coastal Dorset. The bay makes a handsome sweep from the Purbeck peninsula to Ballard Point. Most of the larger hotels are at the northern end of the bay and a 20-minute walk from the town centre. Historic Swanage was a small town relying on the excavation of Portland and Purbeck limestone until the arrival of the steam age and its accompanying tourists in the middle of the last century. The town then developed into the quiet, unassuming resort which remains today.

There is a pleasant walk around the town centre which takes about an hour. Begin at the Alfred monument by the beach in Shore road next to the Mowlem centre. King Alfred – he of the burning cakes – won a resounding maritime victory over the Danes in the bay in 877. The Mowlem recalls John Mowlem, a quarryboy who founded the construction empire which still bears his name.

The seafront Parade leads to the Square and the Stone Quay where the quarry companies shipped their wares. The tramlines in the street were used for stone trucks, not passenger trams. Pleasure boats still depart from the New Pier a little further along. Walk to the end of the bay where there is a coastguard lookout. The Wellington Clock Tower passed on the way was originally brought from Victorian London to decorate the new resort. Then follow Peveril Point Road across the Downs back into the old town, with its attractive pubs and restaurants. The 17th-century façade of the Town Hall was bought from Mercers Hall in London and brought here by a member of the Mowlem family. In neighbouring Town Hall Lane is a tiny temporary prison built in 1803. The old station, built when the branch line from Wareham was opened in 1885, is just around the corner. British Rail abandoned the town in 1972 but the station has been bought privately and now houses a railway centre and museum. Steam trains run on a short section of the line throughout the year at weekends and on weekdays during the summer. There is a good view of the town and the bay from the war memorial on the cliffs behind the Tourist Information Centre in Shore Road.

The Durlston Country Park, which lies behind Swanage on the Purbeck peninsula, can easily engulf a day of fascinating walking. There are spectacular cliff walks and a wide variety of birds, butterflies and plants. A man-made attraction is a vast hunk of local limestone carved into a globe. There is a good information centre and several picnic areas have been created.

A narrow channel of water separates the Isle of Purbeck from Poole, but do not resort to the long main road, through Wareham, for the journey east. A little ferry takes motor traffic across the channel daily and the reward is a journey into the wonderful countryside of Studland which lies on the north east of Purbeck, around Studland Bay. This is a pretty little village surrounded by gorgeous countryside and vast unoccupied beaches, a good introduction to the continental charms of the holiday area of Poole. There is a hefty Norman church, a few local

B&B establishments and one unusual hotel catering for long-stay family holidays. The walks, both by the sea and through woodland, are superb and there are two photogenic rock structures known as Old Harry and Old Harry's Wife. The headland leading to the ferry is under the control of the National Trust which charges a fee for cars using the road. There is easy parking along the way for those who wish to explore the sand dunes and beaches.

Poole

The ferry from Studland arrives at Sandbanks, a tiny peninsula leading to Poole and Bournemouth which marks the end of the rugged, unspoilt Dorset coastline. Modern Poole and Bournemouth now blend into each other imperceptibly to form one continuous community running past Hengistbury Head to the east and into Christchurch Bay.

Bournemouth is a resort town little more than a century old. The beaches are excellent and the town stands behind a line of cliffs broken by the occasional chine, small ravines which lead to the waterfront. It is a busy, open modern place easy on the eye but of little enduring interest. The exception, for lovers of the Romantic poets and Gothic horrors, will be the place's somewhat tenuous connection with Shelley and the creator of one of the best-known monsters of fiction. The poet's wife, Mary Wollstonecraft Shelley, who wrote *Frankenstein*, settled briefly in Bournemouth before her death. She is buried in the churchyard of St Stephen's with her husband's heart. Her home is now a museum.

Poole, on the other hand, should not be mistaken for a modern, purpose-built tourist resort. It is an historic town and one offering constant interest and enjoyment. More boisterous than Swanage, more characterful than Bournemouth, it busies itself around the magnificent Poole Harbour all year round in the pursuit of solid pleasures... food, countryside and boats. The atmosphere is more akin to a continental maritime town than a resort on the south coast of England and attracts hardened Poole addicts back weekend after weekend.

The complex natural harbour, with its patterns of inlets and small coves, is simply magnificent, providing 100 miles of shoreline and a safe inlet for the pleasure boats which throng its waters. It was its provision of a safe haven for marine trades which led to the town's initial development in the 12th century. Some 400 years later it had become one of the most important fishing ports in Britain, despatching craft to the

Poole Custom's House, Dorset

far reaches of the northern Atlantic for fish and trading along the whole of the Mediterranean. Unlike most old ports, Poole retains its original maritime quarter largely unspoilt. Behind the Quay lie historic streets and houses reflecting the styles of many centuries, from Tudor to Georgian, while the waterfront area has been renovated with commendable taste to become a popular focal point for visitors.

The Maritime Museum, in the 15th-century Town Cellars, reflects the ancient trade of the town, displaying exhibits from the Armada, the Bounty voyage, and local smuggling exploits. A nearby medieval merchant's house, Scaplen's Court, has been turned into a museum of everyday life displaying household objects and costumes from several centuries. The Guildhall Museum, in the Georgian Market House and Guildhall, has collections on local history and a magic lantern show of Victorian and Edwardian Poole. A pleasant half day can be spent wandering around these well-kept museums, inspecting the interesting old streets behind the Quay and enjoying the fresh seafood of the local pubs.

The water is never far away. Pleasure boats from the Quay venture out into the far reaches of the harbour on birdwatching outings and there is a regular service to Brownsea Island, in the hands of the National Trust, which is popular with both ornithologists and picnickers. The island is home to ducks, geese and heron and has a small place in the history books; it was here, in 1907, that Lord Baden Powell held a small outdoor camp for boys. It was to lead to the beginning of the Scout and Guide movement.

Sea angling, diving, windsurfing, yachting and boardsailing facilities await those who seek them, and each year the town is host to major sailing competitions and the annual spectacle of the Needles Trophy International Powerboat Weekend, held towards the end of August. Accommodation can be in short supply during competitions. A greater contrast with Lyme's quiet, unassuming pleasures would be hard to imagine, but Poole is no less enjoyable for that.

Tourist Information

The Guildhall
Bridge Street
Lyme Regis
Tel: 02974 2138

7 Acland Road
Dorchester
Tel: 0305 67992

Pavilion Theatre Complex
Weymouth
Tel: 0305 785747

The White House
Shore Road
Swanage
Tel: 0929 422885

Enefco House
Poole Quay
Poole
Tel: 0202 823406

Hotels

Mariners
Silver Street
Lyme Regis
Dorset
Tel: 02974 2753
Quaint hotel used by Beatrix Potter in her paintings.
Rooms: 16
Credit cards: Access, Visa, Amex, Diners
Rating ****

Devon Hotel
Uplyme
Lyme Regis
Dorset
Tel: 02974 3231
Country house in 10 acres of gardens close to the Devon border and a mile from the sea. Closed January to March.

Rooms: 21
Credit cards: Access, Visa, Amex, Diners
Rating ***

The Grand
Burlington Road
Swanage
Dorset
Tel: 0929 423353
Renovated classic Victorian seaside resort hotel with views over Swanage Bay.
Rooms: 30
Credit cards: Access, Visa, Amex, Diners
Rating ***

Salterns Hotel
38 Salterns Way
Lilliput
Poole
Dorset
Tel: 0202 707321
Quiet modern hotel close to the harbour.
Rooms: 16
Credit cards: Access, Visa, Amex, Diners
Rating ***

Highcliff Hotel
St Michael's Road
West Cliff
Bournemouth
Dorset
Tel: 0202 302442
Superb position on clifftop for busy holiday hotel.
Rooms: 110
Credit cards: Access, Visa, Amex, Diners
Rating ***

The Mansion House
Thames Street
Poole
Dorset
Tel: 0202 685666
Luxurious but expensive Georgian mansion close to the Quay. Superb food.
Rooms: 28
Credit cards: Access, Visa, Amex, Diners
Rating *****

Ilchester Arms
Abbotsbury
Dorset
Tel: 0305 871243
Traditional coaching inn in the lovely
village of Abbotsbury, a mile from Chesil
Beach.
Rooms: 9
Credit cards: Access, Visa
Rating ***

Private Accommodation

Maiden Newton House
Nr Dorchester
Dorset
Tel: 0300 20336
Victorian rectory with 21 acres of
grounds and fine home cooking in
elegant dining room. Closed January.
Rooms: 5
Credit cards: Access, Visa
Rating ***

Restaurants

The Galley
9 High Street
Swanage
Tel: 0929 427299
One of the best fish restaurants in the
area, with imaginative cooking bearing
the mark of English, French and oriental
influences. Booking essential.
Credit cards: Access, Visa, Amex
Rating ***

John B's
20 High Street
Poole
Tel: 0202 672440
Ignore the kitsch Edwardian decor –
John B's offers superb food, beautifully
presented. Fixed price menus with daily
specials, much classical French cuisine.
Highly recommended.

Credit cards: Access, Visa, Amex
Rating ****

Mez Creis
16 High Street
Poole
Tel: 0202 674970
Extremely popular fish and seafood
restaurant famous for its platters of
seafood. Booking is advisable in summer.
Closed Sundays.
Credit cards: Access, Visa
Rating ***

Fishnets
Old Mill Suite
The Quay
Poole
Tel 0202 670066
Fixed price cold table and seafood.
Credit cards: Access, Visa
Rating ***

Historic Houses

Clouds Hill (NT)
1m N Bovington Camp
9m E Dorchester
The former cottage home of T.E.
Lawrence (Lawrence of Arabia), with the
famous owner's furnishings. Opening
hours vary, check with tourist
information centre. Closed Tuesdays and
Saturdays.

Corfe Castle (NT)
Corfe
Dramatic ruins of historic fortress
reduced to rubble by Cromwell after a
famous defence. Open daily 10-4.30
February to October, Saturday and
Sunday afternoon only for the rest of the
year.

Thomas Hardy's Cottage (NT)
Melstock Lane
Higher Bockhampton
Hardy's birthplace in 1840. Entry to the
garden only. Open March to October 11-
5.30, Tuesday 2-5.30.

Kingston Lacy House (NT)
Wimborne
The house has one of the best private
picture collections in the country with
works by Van Dyck, Titian, Rubens,
Reynolds and Velasquez. Beautiful
landscaped gardens. Open March to
October 1-4.30, closed Thursdays and
Fridays.

Tudor House
3 Trinity Street
Weymouth
Authentically furnished 17th-century
merchant's house. Open June to
September Wednesday and Thursday
11-4.30.

Gardens

Compton Acres
Canford Cliffs Road
Poole
Rare and sub-tropical plants displayed in
Japanese, Italian, Roman and water
gardens begun in 1919. Daily from April
to October 10.30-6.30 or dusk.

Museums

Nothe Fort
Barrack Road
Weymouth
Museum of coastal defence housed in a
Victorian fort built to protect Portland
Harbour. Period military costumes, 19th-
century cannons and good views of the
harbour and Dorset coastline. Open daily

from 11am to dusk in summer, Sunday
afternoons only in winter.

Corfe Castle Museum
Corfe Castle
Tel: 0929 480921
Local exhibits including dinosaur
footprints. Open daily 9-7.

Dinosaur Museum
Icen Way
Dorchester
Devoted to the wealth of local prehistoric
finds of dinosaur remains and fossils.
Open daily 10-5.30.

Dorset County Museum
High Street West
Dorchester
Superb country museum which has twice
won the Museum of the Year Award.
Reconstruction of Hardy's writing room
and local collections. Open Mondays to
Fridays 10-5, Saturdays 10-1, 2-5.

Dorset Military Museum
The Keep
Bridport Road
Dorchester
Medals and military regalia of local
regiments. Open July to September
Mondays to Saturdays 9-1, 2-5; October to
June Saturdays only, 9-12.

Museum and Art Gallery
South Street
Bridport
Records of unusual local rope industry
and bygones. Open June to September
weekdays ex. Thursday afternoon.

Big Four Railway Museum
81 Old Christchurch Road
Bournemouth
Leading railway museum with exhibits
from the heyday of steam. Monday to
Saturday 10-5, closed Bank Holidays.

Casa Magni Shelley Museum
Boscombe Manor
Beechwood Avenue
Bournemouth
The house of Shelley's wife, Mary,
author of *Frankenstein*, now devoted to
the poet and his era. Monday to Saturday
10-5, June to September; Thursdays,
Fridays and Saturdays the rest of the
year.

Russell-Coates Art Gallery & Museum
Russell-Coates Road
East Cliff
Bournemouth
Paintings, ceramics and theatrical items in
an attractive turn-of-the-century villa.
Mondays to Saturdays 10.30-5.30.

Transport Museum
Mallard Road
Castle Lane
Bournemouth
The town's old trolleybuses and other old
forms of transport. Wednesdays 10.30-5
summer only.

Maritime Museum
The Quay
Poole
Interesting exhibits on the Armada,
Bounty mutiny and local wrecks in a
15th-century building known as the
Town Cellars. Mondays to Saturdays 10-
5, Sunday 2-5.

Guildhall Museum
Market Street
Poole
Comprehensive town museum with
magic lantern show of Victorian and
Edwardian Poole. Mondays to Saturdays
10-5, Sundays 2-5.

Scaplen's Court
High Street
Poole

Medieval merchant's house close to the
Quay recording social history of town:
working kitchen, home furniture and
toys. Mondays to Saturdays 10-1 and 2-5.

Wildlife Parks and Reserves

Durlston Country Park
Swanage
Superb 281-acre country park on the
south eastern corner of the Isle of
Purbeck. Paths and guided walks with
information centre and warden service.
Anvil Point Lighthouse, the Globe, 40 tons
of Portland stone carved into a model of
the world, and the folly of Durlston
Castle are popular points; there is also a
farmland trail.

Thorncombe Wood
nr Dorchester
A 65-acre wood and heath country park
with walks of varying lengths, crossed
by the old roman road and close to
Hardy's birthplace. Signposted at Higher
and Lower Bockhampton.

Brownsea Island (NT)
Poole Harbour
The 500-acre island in the harbour is
reached by regular ferries from the quay.
Brownsea Castle is closed to the public,
but the island has excellent walks and
picnic areas. Red squirrel, wildfowl,
waders and herons are among the
wildlife. Guided tours are available –
inquire at the tourist information centre.

Lodmoor Country Park
Preston Road
Weymouth
Part nature reserve, part tourist
attraction, this 350-acre site encompasses
wildlife, a steam railway, shire horses,
butterfly farm and a sealife centre. Open
daily.

**Radipole Lake Nature Reserve and
Swannery
Weymouth**
A nature reserve managed by the RSPB
in the centre of Weymouth. Wildfowl,
waders and warblers are among the
seasonal visitors. The reserve is open to
the public daily. Information centre, in
the approach to the Swannery car park, is
open April to October daily 10-5; in
winter 10-4 closed Fridays.

**Swanage Railway
Swanage**
Tel: 0929 425800
Private reconstruction of the line from
the Isle of Purbeck to the main Waterloo-
Weymouth route. Currently a six mile
round trip by steam engine.

Walks

The Dorset Coastal Path is the shortest of
the four sections of the South West
Peninsula Coastal Path, running from
Lyme Regis to Poole Harbour. Allow five
days to complete the Dorset path, which
has little hard walking. The path is
signposted throughout its length, but a
good local map is advisable.

Other Diversions

Harvey Yellow Pleasure Boats
Fish Shambles Steps
Poole Quay
Ferry boats to Brownsea Island from the
Quay, the Ferryway, Sandbanks, and
Rockley Sands Caravan Park. Harbour
cruises and ferry to Studland Heath from
Sandbanks.

Robert Hale Pleasure Boats
Custom House Steps
Poole Quay
Ferry service to Brownsea Island and
cruises on to Wareham.

4 North Dorset

Inland Dorset offers an escape route from the crowds on the coast. Many of the villages and towns have connections with Hardy and his books: quiet country places of great charm and beauty. Shaftesbury is a lovely hilltop town with a famous cobbled street, Gold Hill. Blandford Forum is a classical Georgian market town, while Sherborne is famous both for its abbey and castle and its public schools. Cerne Abbas has its famous hillside giant cut into the chalk and is one of the most pleasant villages in the region. The inland towns are within easy reach of the coast or can be combined with visits to east Devon or Somerset. Accommodation is mainly at inns or bed and breakfast establishments in or near the principal towns. There are few chain hotels in the area. This is a perfect place for a weekend break. Only one base is needed to see all of the principal sights, and the distances are modest. Even two or three days will fit in rewarding visits and time for walks in the magnificent Dorset countryside.

Cerne Abbas

The village of Cerne Abbas lies on the road from Dorchester to Sherborne and must count as one of the high points of the new visitor's tour of Dorset. It is a delightful place in itself; the presence of the mysterious Cerne Giant cut into the hill overlooking the village makes a startling, barbarian backdrop to the elegant little village.

The giant, a naked figure 180 feet high wielding a club and rather over-optimistically physically endowed, is a local conundrum. Carved figures can be seen elsewhere in Britain though they are normally less explicit. Representations of gods, kings and creatures – the ubiquitous white horse being the most familiar of the latter – have existed since earliest times, and there are some who believe that the Cerne giant depicts the ancient hero Hercules.

The odd thing about the giant is that there is no mention whatsoever of his existence until the 18th century. Was there an earlier representation which was revived by the villagers of that time? Or had the figure simply escaped mention in the many earlier books which documented contemporary Dorset? The latter theory is certainly hard to believe. The giant's presence on the hill overlooking Cerne is so predominant that it could hardly have escaped the notice of the chroniclers of the time.

The notion which appeals to this writer most – and there is no evidence to the contrary – is that the 18th-century inhabitants of Cerne, labelled as 'moste unorderlie governed and as unruiellie as if there were noe magistrates' by an earlier official report, took it upon themselves to carve the giant anew, whether from earlier plans or simply from scratch. Since that day, their descendants have regularly maintained the chalk outline, a considerable task since, left untended, the grass will cover the giant's figure in a few short years, winning a good measure of fame for their village and no small income from curious travellers. How the giant's frank nakedness escaped the attention of the prudish Victorians is quite beyond me. People who felt moved to cover the legs of dining tables lest they move beholders to lustful feelings must have felt quite giddy when their eyes alighted on the Cerne Giant. Ever more mysteries... one hopes that the curious archeologists never uncover the truth for it may be too mundane to contemplate.

Cerne Abbas

Another reason why the giant

surely did not stand in all his splendour in earlier times is that, for several centuries from 987 onwards, the village housed an active Benedictine monastery. You can still see some of the remaining ruins today. Could such a querulous and notetaking community have failed to have noted, in their interminable annals, the presence of the wild figure overlooking their abbey? Even though he might not have been a suitable subject for an illuminated manuscript, I find this doubtful. No, there is good old Dorset trickery behind the Cerne Giant, and I suspect several of the tight-lipped villagers of today know the truth behind this tale (and pray that they keep it to themselves).

The village itself is beautifully preserved. There is a set of village stocks, from the days when miscreants were punished publicly, a village duck pond, some splendid medieval buildings and a handsome 14th-century church. The village lacks a hotel, and is probably grateful for the deficiency, but the Red Lion is a classic country pub of Tudor origins for lunch or an early evening drink.

Sherborne

For a scenic route to Sherborne, branch right, past the giant, then continue north. On a clear day, the view extends over the Vale of Blackmoor. Then rejoin the main Dorchester-Sherborne road at Middlemarsh, crossing the River Yeo to reach North Dorset's largest town.

Sherborne, in the popular mind, inevitably spells public school. In fact, there are two schools, for both sexes; the boys' was founded by Edward VI. Both are educational establishments of world renown and occupy prominent buildings in the town, the boys' school being partly situated in what remains of the old abbey. Sherborne is a grand, open place of fine houses and indefinable Dorset character. The town's most famous resident was Sir Walter Raleigh who occupied the old castle given to him by Elizabeth. This was when relations between the two were cordial and the explorer famous for his travels to the New World which brought back potatoes and tobacco. The great man was later to fall out of favour, losing Sherborne. He was imprisoned for conspiracy under the reign of James I and beheaded in 1616.

The ruins of the old castle, which was built in the 12th century, lie to the south of the town. Close by stands the current castle, begun by Raleigh when he found that he could not improve the original structure

Monks Washing Place on Pack Monday, Sherborne

to his satisfaction. Sherborne Castle has been occupied by the Digby family since the early 17th century and is now one of the principal privately-owned stately homes of inland Dorset that is open to the public. The 1,000-acre estate includes 20 acres of deer park designed by Capability Brown.

There is evidence that the Romans had a small settlement here, building villas along the banks of the Yeo. The town was also a Saxon settlement of some importance. In the early 8th century, the Saxon kingdom established a cathedral in the town and this remained the centre of church power until Norman times when the bishopric moved to Old Sarum. The lovely abbey church at the heart of the town is mainly 15th century but contains some earlier work by Norman and Saxon hands. Former abbey buildings now serve as classrooms for the boys' school and the old gatehouse houses the town museum. There are pleasant villages in virtually every direction but two deserve special mention, Over and Nether Compton close to the county border which both possess particularly fine medieval churches.

Blandford Forum

Two interesting roads lead east from Sherborne, one to the picturesque hillside town of Shaftesbury, the second to Blandford Forum. There is no easy circuit of inland Dorset to be made from this point. The traveller can easily absorb a day in the villages and countryside of the north or south, but it may be rushing matters to combine the two into a single journey.

The shortest route to Blandford is to follow the A3030/357 by Sturminster Newton. A more circuitous path briefly retraces the A352 towards Dorchester then branches off to the B3146 to run alongside the Piddle river, a slightly risqué name which was often changed in Victorian times to Puddle. This is a most attractive route, away from the beaten path, ending at the village of Puddletown. Thorncombe Wood, see p. 80, and Puddletown Forest are good walking country and the village has a pretty square.

A few miles along the main A35 trunk road from here lies Tolpuddle, home of the famous martyrs who are commemorated in a trade union museum. This pretty little village, sited by the Piddle with a 13th-century church and picturebook agricultural cottages, seems a strange location for a shrine to trade unionism. That it took the part in trade union

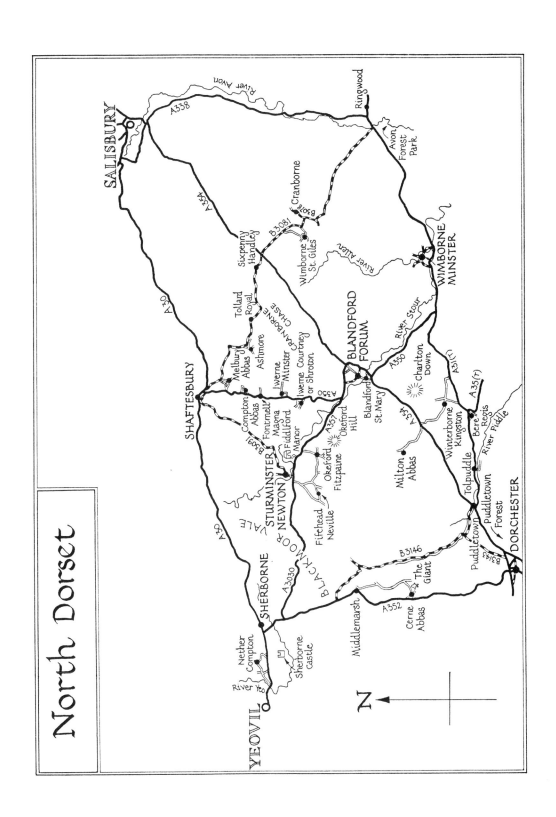

North Dorset

history it did is an indication of the severe poverty in rural Dorset during the early part of the 19th century. In 1830 and 1831 riots in nearby Bere Regis had frightened the landowners who controlled the lives of thousands of agricultural workers through property and price and wage fixing. It was in this atmosphere that the six Tolpuddle labourers were brought to court in Dorchester to face charges of breaking the Unlawful Oaths Act, a piece of legislation designed to prevent the formation of trade unions and 'secret societies' intended to challenge the power of the landowning class. The unlawful oath was simply a pledge to jointly challenge any attempt by the landowners to reduce wages.

The Tolpuddle six were found guilty and transported to Australia for seven years. But their case caused an outcry throughout the country and became a *cause célèbre* for those supporting the formation of a legitimate trade union movement. The Tolpuddle Martyrs are still remembered at an annual trade union rally in the village each year. A small museum tells their story, and the 'Martyrs' Tree', under which they are said to have met, is still preserved.

Bere Regis, a few miles along the A35, has a lovely church with a memorial to the Turberville family whose name was used by Hardy for his famous story of *Tess of the d'Urbervilles*. To the north is Milton Abbas, a village of thatched cottages which has appeared in many an English country calendar. The Milton Abbey House, a public school on the site of a Saxon monastery, has an unusual grass staircase of 111 steps, open to the public daily, which leads to its chapel.

A minor road after Bere turns left, over Charlton Down and past Winterborne Kingston, rejoining the A354 for the last few miles into Blandford Forum, a gem of Georgian architecture in a lovely setting by the River Stour. The town was almost totally destroyed by fire in 1731. Over the next 30 years it was rebuilt along strict Georgian lines by two local brothers, John and William Bastard, to a plan which has been preserved to this day, making Blandford one of the most perfect small towns of its era in the country. The architectural uniformity of Blandford has been scarcely disturbed for two centuries, though traffic frequently throngs the streets and Saturdays are best avoided by drivers. There is an attractive parish church and town hall, and, in the Market Place, a classical monument to mark the fire which shaped the town. The unique history of Blandford is recounted at the town museum in Bere's Yard. A more unusual museum is that of the Royal Signals Regiment, at nearby Blandford Camp, which tells the history of military communications and the Royal Signals.

Blandford is best explored on foot, with no particular itinerary. The place is small enough to be seen in one afternoon, or there is accommodation at the handsome Crown Hotel. One local speciality should be sampled: Badger Beer, brewed by Hall and Woodhouse in neighbouring Blandford St Mary, a traditional English ale of the kind beloved by Hardy.

Shaftesbury

Two routes north lead to Shaftesbury from Blandford. The shortest, along the A350, passes the three interesting villages of the Iwernes, each of which has an interesting church. Iwerne Minster most merits a visit, with its large church of Norman origins and several attractive old houses. Fontmell Magna, a little further north, is as pretty as its name, a small village with thatched cottages in a conservation area, with a converted mill now serving as a pottery. Near Compton Abbas, some 800 feet above sea level on the hills of Cranborne Chase, is a small airfield from which visitors can, for a reasonable sum, persuade the pilots of the flying school to embark on a pleasure flight of 30 minutes or so. On a clear day this is magnificent flying country in a light aircraft, with wonderful views to Salisbury and its cathedral, the coast and Shaftesbury, perched on its hill. The airfield also has a restaurant of some reputation, with candlelit dining in the evenings.

A longer route from Blandford is to take the Sherborne road (A357) then head north at Sturminster Newton. Before Sturminster is Fiddleford Mill with its English Heritage medieval manor house. Sturminster itself is a pretty little town on the banks of the Stour in the Vale of Blackmoor, home of one of the busiest cattle markets in the county. There is a medieval bridge with six arches across the Stour, several attractive streets and a handsome town square. Sturminster's fortunes once rested on the wool trade. It was an important clothmaking town supplying the military. Today, agriculture is the principal trade, and the town retains that individual county character which is so remarkable of Dorset. The county's second greatest poet, William Barnes, was born here, and Hardy made it his home for two years. Barnes, who wrote in county dialect, is little known today and much of his work, for the newcomer, is unreadable. For much of the 19th century, he was the county's foremost literary figure until, at the end of his life, he was eclipsed by Hardy.

Shaftesbury (View across Blackmoor Vale)

South of Sturminster, two lovely villages demand a detour for those who have the time. Okeford Fitzpaine, with a medieval village cross and church, is a picture postcard image of thatched cottages. It adjoins the 19-acre Okeford Hill where there is a walk to the top of Bulbarrow Hill, 902 feet above sea level, from which the Bristol Channel can be seen on clear days, and a picnic site. Nearby Fifehead Neville is another pretty village, with a medieval church and the remains of a Roman villa excavated in Victorian times.

From Sturminster, Shaftesbury is a short drive away along the B3091. Of all North Dorset's admirable features, Shaftesbury is among the finest, set some 700 feet above sea level on a bluff that has been occupied by man since he first came to south west England. Alfred, the hero king of Wessex, knew Shaftesbury well and established a nunnery here, with his own daughter as its first abbess. The famous King Canute died here. It was briefly a centre of pilgrimage when the body of Edward the Martyr – murdered at Corfe Castle – was reburied here in the 10th century, until the more colourful shrines of Glastonbury and Canterbury captured the medieval imagination. The wealth that Shaftesbury pilgrimage and clerical bureaucracy brought to Shaftesbury naturally made it a target during the Dissolution. Henry VIII's men tore the abbey apart and used the stone for building work. Today, only a few tantalising ruins from the old abbey remain to give a glimpse of the grandeur of nearly a millennium ago.

High on its windy hill, Shaftesbury has commanding views as far as Glastonbury Tor. The best-known sight in the town, however, is Gold Hill, a cobbled street set at an angle of seemingly impractical steepness. When the advertising industry was looking for a street which could exemplify the image of the north of England, it turned, incongruously, to Gold Hill. With a voiceover of suitably dropped aitches, the hill was turned into 'the Hovis street' of popular renown.

The sights of Shaftesbury deserve an afternoon. Walk around the old part of the town, taking in the gardens of Park Walk and Castle Hill. The local history museum, in Gold Hill, documents some of the town's glorious past, and there is a model of Shaftesbury at the time of the dissolution in the abbey museum in Park Walk.

Cranborne Chase

Shaftesbury is at the very eastern edge of Dorset. The county boundary with Wiltshire lies just to the east of the town, where the busy A30 leads directly to Salisbury, running along the northern foot of the Cranborne Chase hills. By far the most interesting route out of the town is along the B3081 minor road which runs across the Chase to join the A354 Blandford to Salisbury road.

Cranborne Chase became a royal hunting forest under King John and remained so until the 17th century. It is now wild and unspoilt, designated as an area of outstanding natural beauty, with chalkland hills almost 1,000 feet above sea level and views to the Isle of Wight and the Mendips. Deer continue to graze on the hills, now safe from royal hunters. There are opportunities for walks, long and short, along the length of the Chase.

Melbury Abbas, on the outskirts of Shaftesbury off the minor road, is an interesting little place with mills along the length of the village stream. Zigzag Hill takes the motorist to the heights of the Chase, briefly crossing into Wiltshire.

Ashmore, at the summit of the Chase, is Dorset's highest village. There is, unexpectedly, a large village pond which never runs dry; around it there is an annual fair with country dancing on the Friday closest to Midsummer's Day. With a scattering of thatched cottages and a handsome village church, Ashmore is as photogenic as many better known Dorset hamlets. Tollard Royal, on the Wiltshire side of the Chase, has a medieval mansion known as King John's House reputed to have been used as a royal hunting lodge. After Sixpenny Handley, once again in Dorset, the road joins the main Blandford to Salisbury trunk road.

If there is time, it is worth briefly following the minor road a little further. Cranborne has a 12th-century church with some original wall paintings remaining. Neighbouring Wimborne St Giles is a fetching village which has been in the hands of the earls of Shaftesbury since the 15th century. Several generations of the family are remembered in the 18th-century village church.

Tourist Information

(* denotes a seasonal service only)

Hound Street
Sherborne*
Tel: 0935 815341

Marsh & Ham car park
Blandford Forum*
Tel: 0258 51989

Bell Street
Shaftesbury
Tel: 0747 3514

Hotels

Eastbury
Long Street
Sherborne
Dorset
Tel: 0935 813131
Georgian town house hotel with walled garden.
Rooms: 12
Credit cards: Access, Visa, Amex
Rating ***

Crown Hotel
1 West Street
Blandford Forum
Tel: 0258 56626
Attractive Georgian hotel close to the centre of town.
Rooms: 28
Credit cards: Access, Visa, Amex, Diners
Rating ****

Royal Chase
Royal Chase Roundabout
Shaftesbury
Dorset
Tel: 0747 53355
Country hotel in grounds near the busy A30 Salisbury trunk road. Indoor pool.

Rooms: 31
Credit cards: Access, Visa, Amex, Diners
Rating ****

Plumber Manor
Sturminster Newton
Tel: 0258 72507
Jacobean mansion owned by the same family since the early 17th century. Free stabling for guests who want to hunt with the local packs.
Rooms: 6
Credit cards: Access, Visa
Rating ****

Fiddleford Inn
Fiddleford
Sturminster Newton
Dorset
Tel: 0258 72489
Village inn dating from the 18th century in lovely countryside.
Rooms: 5
Credit cards; Access, Visa
Rating **

Private Accommodation

The Old Rectory
St James
Shaftesbury
Dorset
Tel: 0747 52003
Beautiful 18th-century house half a mile from the centre of Shaftesbury.
Rooms: 2
Credit cards: none
Rating **

Restaurants

Plumber Manor
Sturminster Newton
Tel: 0258 72507
Fixed price menus, dinner only in marvellous country mansion. Modern

Plumber Manor contd
cooking with French influences by Brian
Prideaux-Brune.
Rooms: 6
Credit cards: Access, Visa
Rating ****

The Courtyard
Long Street
Sherborne
Tel: 0935 814080
Imaginative cooking – hare and duck
with plums are examples – from local
produce. Outdoor tables in fine weather.
Closed Mondays.
Credit cards: Access, Visa
Rating ***

Historic Houses

Sherborne Castle
Sherborne
Built by Walter Raleigh in 1594 close to
the original castle, now in ruins (see
Ancient Monuments). Beautiful parkland
with 20 acres of lawns, wooded walks
and a 50-acre lake, still in the hands of the
Digby family who have lived in the castle
since 1617. Open from Easter Saturday
until the end of September, Thursdays,
Saturdays, Sundays and Bank Holiday
Mondays 2-5.30 only. Grounds only 12
noon to 6 Saturdays, Sundays, Bank
Holiday Mondays and 1.30-6 on
Thursdays.

Ancient Monuments

Sherborne Old Castle (EH)
Sherborne
Ruins of 12th-century castle destroyed by
Cromwell after a 16-day siege; 'a
malicious and mischievous castle, like its
owner', Cromwell declared. Once the
home of Walter Raleigh. Open daily 10-6
summer, 10-4 and closed Mondays
winter.

Fiddleford Manor (EH)
1m E Sturminster Newton
Manor house with 14th- and 17th-century
parts and attractive hall.
Open daily 10-6.

Museums

Blandford Forum Museum
Bere's Yard
Market Place
Blandford Forum
Illustration of the life and culture of
Blandford. Open 10.30-12.30 and 2.30-4.30.

Royal Signals Museum
Blandford Camp
Blandford Forum
Museum of the Royal Signals. Open
9-4.30 Monday to Friday.

Local History Museum
Gold Hill
Shaftesbury
Open Easter to September weekdays 11-5,
Sundays 2.30-5.

Abbey Ruins and Museum
Park Walk
Shaftesbury
Relics from the Abbey ruins and
medieval town model. Open Tuesday to
Sunday, Easter to September.

Sherborne Museum
Abbey Gate House
Sherborne
Exhibits on the local silk industry as well
as the usual regional displays. Open April
to October 10.30-12.30 and 3-4.30,
Tuesdays to Saturdays; 3-5 on Sundays.
Winter, Tuesdays and Saturdays only,
10.30-12.30 and 3-4.30.

Tolpuddle Martyr's Museum
Tolpuddle
Tel: 0305 84237
Devoted to the memory of the early
trade unionist deportees to Australia.
Open daily 9-4 in winter and 9-6 in
summer.

Wildlife Parks and Reserves

Avon Forest Park
2m W Ringwood
A 580-acre park of mixed heath and pine
woodland with walks and picnic areas,
views over the Avon valley.

Other Diversions

Compton Abbas Airfield
Compton Abbas
Tel: 0747 811767
Pleasure flights over the glorious Dorset
countryside... marvellous in fine
weather. The airfield has a popular
licenced restaurant.

Glastonbury Tor

5 Somerset

Visitors to Somerset normally head for Exmoor and the coast around Minehead. Wessex encompasses the inland part of the county, running south west from Wells to the border with Devon, a largely rural area of small ancient towns and the rich, natural flatland of the Somerset Levels. The M5 motorway follows the route to Taunton and beyond into Devon but can be severely congested during the peak periods of summer. Quiet country roads are slower but more rewarding. There are good independent hotels and small guesthouses throughout the region. The principal places to stay are the small cathedral city of Wells, Glastonbury with its Arthurian connections and busy Taunton which, in the Castle, can boast one of the finest hotels in Wessex. Bristol, Wiltshire and Dorset are easily reached from the Wells and Glastonbury area while the south can be linked with trips into east Devon or the Dorset coast (see pp. 61-81, 117-31). There are several good vineyards in the area which can be combined to make a wine trail; they are listed at the end of the section. Somerset has much to see; a weekend break will only encompass half of the county. Plan on a leisurely week, preferably with bases in the north and south of the county, to make the most of your visit.

Wells

In north east Somerset stand the Mendip Hills which rise near the coast at Weston-super-Mare and run east inland to Shepton Mallet. One of the most attractive routes into the region is from the north, crossing the Mendips, along the A39 or A37, and leading to Wells.

Wells can boast that it is the smallest cathedral city in Britain, and what a fine cathedral it is. The city is the best possible introduction to inland Somerset, beautiful, individual and historic. After seeing Wells, the lesser sights of the county fall into better perspective.

The city sits at the foot of the Mendips and has a permanent population of fewer than 10,000 residents, though this number is swollen daily by the busy tourist trade. It owes its fame almost entirely to the patronage of the church and the development of the great cathedral and its related religious bureaucracy. Wells was the original source of religious authority in the region from its establishment in Saxon times. When Bath prospered, the bishopric was united under the name of Bath *and* Wells, and remains so today. Work began on the cathedral in the 12th century and finished in the 14th, providing the hub of a large and influential religious community. From the 14th century onwards, after a fractious dispute between the townspeople and the church, the cathedral and associated clerical buildings were encircled with walls and moated, a virtual church fortress in the centre of the small city. This facility came in useful for the bishop as recently as 1831 when the drawbridge was briefly raised at Wells as a precautionary measure after rioters had destroyed the Bishop's Palace in Bristol. This separation of church from city is largely responsible for the delight of Wells for the modern visitor. The cathedral and its precincts remain a rare and complete picture of a prosperous, medieval religious society.

The city has an attractive High Street with interesting shops. Water from the springs which give Wells its name – located in what is now the garden of the Bishop's Palace – runs down channels each side of the street. The usual entrance to the cathedral area is from the medieval Market Place. The West Front of the cathedral is its greatest exterior asset, a medieval sculpture gallery of 293 statues set in niches which covers the whole of the façade. Inside, there is an unusual early Gothic nave and striking scissor arches which support the weight of the tower, the latter a 14th-century addition to the problem of sinking foundations.

97

The north transept has a clock dating from 1390 which, every quarter of an hour, reveals knights jousting at a tournament. In the south transept there are carvings of everyday medieval life, including two depicting toothache sufferers.

Steps lead to the beautiful Chapter House, the meeting house of the medieval religious bureaucracy. On the east walk of the Cloisters is the Library, begun in 1425 and restored in the 17th century. The Chain Gate, built between 1459 and 1460, leads from the precinct to the delightful Vicars' Close, a fully preserved street of medieval houses unrivalled in Britain. Wells is famous for its choir which may be heard regularly in the

Cheddar Gorge

cathedral and is based in the cathedral school of 700 pupils which occupies buildings in the north of the precinct.

To the south is the Bishop's Palace, surrounded by a moat and walls. The house is private but the gardens are open on Thursdays and Sundays during the summer and well worth the visit.

Wells has a good town museum in the Cathedral Green with collections featuring local natural and social history and the bones of 'the witch of Wookey Hole', a female cavedweller found in the Wookey Hole caves two miles away. The village of Wookey Hole lies along the banks of the River Axe and is now the centre of a considerable tourist industry. Archeologists have uncovered signs of human occupation by prehistoric man in the caves. Modern visitors are treated to a guided tour through the labyrinth of caverns by the owners, Madame Tussaud's, who also operate a fairground art collection and waxworks museum on the site. Wookey's more traditional industry is paper-making; recently the craft has been revived.

To the north west lies Cheddar and more famous caves. The cheese of the area is now of secondary interest to this busy village set against the spectacular backdrop of the Cheddar Gorge. Tourism is the prime industry here today, and the independent visitor should try to avoid summer weekends which can be too fraught for comfort.

The Gorge is one of the most breathtaking sights of Wessex, a dramatic gash through the limestone of the Mendips. There are walks to the cliffs of the Gorge and explorations of the vast network of caves, leisurely or, for the more adventurous, to basic potholing standards. One cheesemaking company opens its doors to visitors to see the process in a modern factory alongside 'Mangel Wurzel's Zider Museum'. For all the tourist ephemera, Cheddar is an ancient place, with traces of a Saxon palace and medieval vestiges around the marketplace. If you intend to walk to the clifftop or spend some time in the caves, allow half a day for your visit. Wookey and Cheddar are, in many ways, rivals, and I doubt that many people would want to combine both cave complexes in one day.

Glastonbury

A new Avalon for ageing hippies, a quirky little Somerset market town, an historic centre of early Christianity in Britain... Glastonbury is all of these, and a busy little tourist centre as well, not too proud to erect the

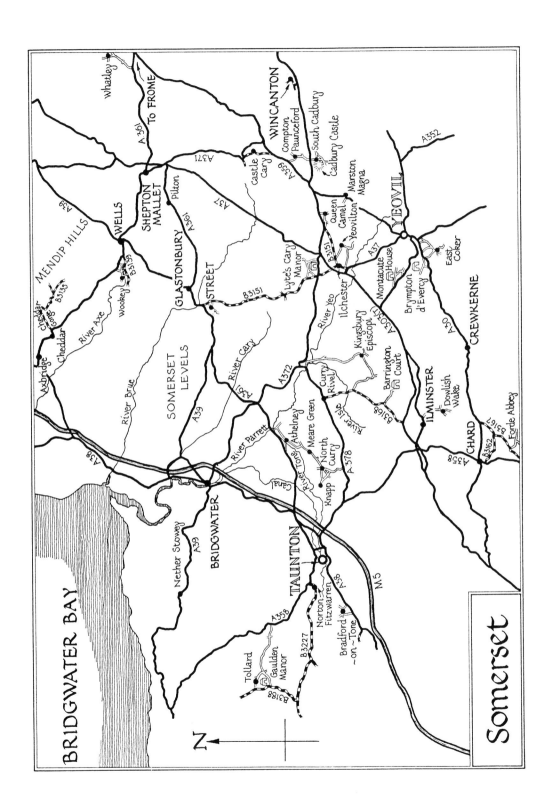

BRIDGWATER BAY

MENDIP HILLS

Cheddar Gorge
Cheddar
Axbridge
Wookey
WELLS
River Axe
River Brue
B3135
B3139
A39
A38
A371
A361
To FROME
Whatley
SHEPTON MALLET
Pilton
A361
A37
GLASTONBURY
STREET
SOMERSET LEVELS
A39
A361
B3151
River Cary
A372
River Parrett
Nether Stowey
A39
BRIDGWATER
Canal
River Tone
Athelney
Meare Green
North Curry
Knapp
A378
River Isle
Curry Rivel
River Yeo
Ilchester
Kingsbury Episcopi
Barrington Court
B3168
Lyte's Cary Manor
B3151
Queen Camel
Yeovilton
A37
Marston Magna
Montacute
Brympton d'Evercy
House
A3088
A303
YEOVIL
East Coker
A30
CREWKERNE
A352
Castle Cary
A359
WINCANTON
Compton Pauncefoot
South Cadbury
Cadbury Castle
ILMINSTER
Dowlish Wake
CHARD
A358
A30
B3162
B3167
Forde Abbey
M5
A38
TAUNTON
A358
Norton Fitzwarren
Bradford ~on~Tone
B3227
Tollard
Gaulden Manor
B3188

N

Somerset

odd Arthur's Wine Bar with the civic tongue very much in cheek. There is nowhere quite like it anywhere else in the country and a memorable visit it makes for those who can take a touch of fake Arthuriana in the right spirit.

The very location of the place lends itself to the mystical connotations which abound here. The town lies under the shadow of the Tor, a sizable hill topped by the tower of St Michael's chapel. In the early morning mist, the Tor resembles a fanciful island straight from the picture books of Arthurian legend, and even the most cynical begin to understand why Glastonbury can exert such a grip on those of an imaginative nature. When the area was first occupied by early man, the Tor was an island, surrounded by treacherous swamps and marshland. The followers of Arthur later claimed it as the site of the mythical Isle of Avalon mentioned in the Arthurian chronicles to which the mortally wounded king was carried after his last battle with Mordred in Cornwall.

It is relatively simple to separate fact from fantasy in Glastonbury, nor does it diminish the place to do so. If you seek the fantastic, there is a plethora of fascinating bookshops to whet your appetite with tales of geomancy, ley lines, the Round Table and other ancient British mysteries. Gothic Image, in the High Street, is a positive Aladdin's Cave of such fare and must be one of the few bookshops in Britain where tomes on feminism share shelf space with extra-terrestrial conspiracy theories and natural histories of the dragon.

The facts are easily summarised. There is evidence that Glastonbury was occupied before the Roman invasion, and indications that early man attached religious significance to the site. Given its eerie location, it would have been extraordinary if he had not. In the seventh century a Saxon monastery was established at the foot of the Tor. This established strong links with Ireland and a reputation among academics. One of its best known figures was St Dunstan, who became abbot in 945 and went on to become Archbishop of Canterbury, leaving Glastonbury richer in lands. The original Saxon church was destroyed by fire in the 12th century and replaced by the Lady Chapel of today.

Until the 12th century, there was no apparent suggestion of any connection between the town and the legendary king Arthur, a figure made popular by ballads and Geoffrey of Monmouth's imaginative 'histories'. Then, in 1191, a grave was discovered which bore the inscription of the mythical king, and the Arthur cult which was to enrich Glastonbury began. The sceptical will conclude that Arthur was simply good for business. Certainly, medieval pilgrimage was an industry for the monastic orders, as organised and calculated as modern day tourism. Watching the crowds queue up in Canterbury for the shrine of Thomas à Becket, the monks of Glastonbury may well have felt that they were letting a good commercial opportunity slip by.

The legend of Arthur appealed to a nationalistic streak in the English character, as it does today. Perhaps the allure of Arthur had waned in the early 13th century. It was around then that Glastonbury gained an even more fantastic connection with the past; the monks 'discovered' evidence that, in AD 37, Joseph of Arimathea had visited the town. This was distinctly adventurous of the chap; the Romans were a good seven years behind him. This tale led Glastonbury to claim that it was the site of the first Christian church in Britain; while most town legends require a pinch of salt, this one demands a positive cellarful. In 1278 Edward I watched as the legendary king's bones were reburied in the choir in front of the High Altar of the abbey.

The cult of Arthur and, to a lesser extent, Joseph enriched the abbey enormously, making it one of the richest in the country. Naturally, this attracted the attention of Henry VIII when he dissolved the monasteries. The then abbot and two of his monks were executed on the Tor for refusing to hand over the abbey treasures, and the great monastic community was destroyed almost overnight, crumbling into ruins.

Today it ranks as one of the more memorable sights of modern Wessex, an atmospheric collection of ruins which, over the centuries, seem to have absorbed the transcendental powers attributed to them by generations of visitors. Arthur's tomb, the underground chapel of Joseph and the site of the high altar are little more than jumbled relics of stone, but they still carry a degree of fascination which belies their physical appearance. But the abbey is better preserved than one might have expected after centuries of neglect. St Mary's Chapel and the Galilee chapel are partly intact and there is a lovely 14th-century abbot's kitchen complete with vaulted domed roof. The only functional religious building remaining is the 16th-century Chapel of St Patrick where communion is celebrated every Tuesday at 10.30am. The abbey is now well looked after by a local trust which has an interesting museum containing fragments of the original Saxon church, Roman remains and a model of the abbey at the peak of its fame.

Do not make the mistake – as do many visitors – of thinking that Glastonbury is the abbey alone. There is much of interest elsewhere. St John's church is a fetching Perpendicular construction of the 15th century, based on Norman origins. There are interesting tombs inside, and the heraldic 'arms' of Joseph of Arimathea in the south window (one longs for a time machine to test whether the good Joseph would have recognised them as such). Outside is one of the town's Glastonbury Thorn trees, a descendant of the tree which mystically grew from Joseph's staff. The thorn, a relative of the hawthorn, flowers twice a year, in spring and winter, and can be found in many gardens locally. From this specimen sprigs are cut each Christmas and sent to the Queen and Queen Mother. The Church of St Benignus marks Glastonbury's Irish connections, being dedicated to a Hibernian saint. It is a lively structure, part 15th-century, part Victorian, with Perpendicular leanings.

Glastonbury High Street has a good share of medieval buildings and a range of shops which reflect the arcane interests of the local population. It does seem a shame that the heavy traffic which mars the road cannot be diverted elsewhere. The Tribunal is the original 15th-century courthouse which now houses a local museum with finds from the Glastonbury Lake Iron Age village, including a dugout boat and an ancient saw. Close by, the George and Pilgrims Hotel, built in the late 15th century by the then abbot, was used as accommodation for pilgrims visiting the shrines of Arthur and Joseph. The front is attractive medieval stone and the interior, at the time of writing, largely unspoilt by the depredations of the modern hotel trade.

In Magdalene Street can be found the little Pump House, now a private home, which was once the focus of the town's short-lived spa trade. It is worth walking to the Chalice Hill, the source of the waters which have had a healing reputation for many centuries. The hill is named after the legend that Joseph of Arimathea hid the chalice from the Last Supper here. The chalice became the sought-after Holy Grail of Arthur's Court. The spring at the Chalice Well flows at a constant rate of 25,000 gallons a day and a constant temperature of 52° Fahrenheit. The area around the well is now maintained by a trust which preserves its natural surroundings. If you wish to drink the waters, do so at the lion's head outlet only, since they may be polluted elsewhere; they are very high in iron content and probably originate in the Mendips.

The two other hills of Glastonbury make for good walking. The famous Tor, with the ruins of St Michael's Church, is now in the hands of the National Trust and harmed by erosion caused by the hundreds of thousands of visitors who trek to the summit each year. The way to the Tor is signposted from the town; there is no car park or obvious parking space nearby. Only the tower remains of St Michael's, which was built in

Somerset Levels

the 14th century and restored in 1804. Weary-All, or Wirrall, Hill, to the west, was once used for the vineyards of the abbey and is said to be the original site of the Glastonbury Thorn.

The Somerset Levels

To the west and south of the town are the Somerset Levels, reclaimed marshland which has been dug for centuries for its rich peat. With the decline of the traditional shoemaking industry in Glastonbury and neighbouring Street, peat digging is one of the few remaining ancient industries of the area. Those who work the peat bogs today have usually learnt the trade from relatives. It is a wild and mysterious region and the persistent, who are willing to buy a few rounds of cider in Glastonbury's working men's pubs, can talk their way onto an early morning trek into the misty marshland. Tales of curious events – disappearances and discoveries of odd graves – abound. One peatman, suitably lubricated with local cider, dismissed all the well-known Glastonbury legends to the author but insisted that somewhere in the peat levels lies a solid gold coffin of a Saxon king which had been briefly sighted once, then lost. 'And I couldn't even find it again with my JCB,' he added.

This may have been a little invention for the gullible visitor, of course, but there is evidence of much activity by ancient man in the Levels. Evidence of prehistoric tracks across the area abound and the *Guinness Book of Records* declares one such track, dated by scientists at around 3,200 BC, to be the oldest road in the world.

The peat trade is one of the rural activities depicted at the Somerset Rural Life Museum, housed in a fine 14th-century stone barn in Bere Lane, close to the Chalice Hill, in Glastonbury. The excellent displays of cidermaking and other farm activities have, deservedly, won the museum several prizes, and there are demonstrations of farm crafts, from beekeeping to cheesemaking, on summer weekends and local entertainments.

The best way to experience the Somerset Levels on foot is to take the Curry Moor Trail which runs for six miles on a circular route beginning from Athelney north east of Taunton. The walk takes in lovely countryside, rich in migratory birds and wintering wildfowl, aquatic and marshland plants and flowers, following the River Tone to Lower Knapp then returning by North Curry and Meare Green. North Curry is a pretty Somerset village, well preserved with a Georgian air. At Meare

Green Court the Willows and Wetlands Visitor Centre is an exhibition describing the willow industry and the life of the wetlands. Visitors can see willow baskets being made at the Willows English Basket Centre in Curload close to Hook Bridge, on the return to Athelney. A leaflet describing the walk in detail is available in local tourist information centres in the area.

From Athelney there is also a shorter walk to the Athelney monument, a mile east of Curload. This was erected in 1801 to mark the place where King Alfred successfully evaded the Danes in 878. At the time, Athelney was an island and parts of the lowlands are still flooded in winter.

Street, almost an extension of Glastonbury, is a town of minor interest but deserving of some mention. This was the home of the Clark brothers, Quakers who built up a great shoemaking industry here from the early 19th century. The company maintains a shoe museum, though most of its manufacturing takes place elsewhere today. Some small companies are still actively involved in shoemaking, and the sheepskin coat business provides a living for several local firms.

Taunton

The A39, then the A361, lead south from Glastonbury to Taunton. Those in a hurry may wish to follow the A39 to the M5, which runs direct all the way to Exeter, but beware of summer weekends when traffic returning from the West Country may choke the motorway solid for many hours.

Taunton is the county town of Somerset, a modern commercial community with a little of the medieval at its heart. The Castle Hotel, one of the best – and the most expensive – in the region, is a good reason for staying here. Most visitors will be able to satisfy their curiosity in half a day and spend the night somewhere more characterful. The place is famous for its associations with cider. Sheppy's, near Bradford-on-Tone, is an excellent old-fashioned cidermaker of great local repute. Better known to the world at large is the Taunton Cider Company (TCC) in Norton Fitzwarren, off the Barnstaple Road. This is the manufacturer of two of the country's best selling ciders, Dry Blackthorn and Autumn Gold. The company was formed in 1911 but was transformed during the 1970s when the world of drinks marketing and advertising came to the cider business. The company, and its rivals, now manufacture a drink that would be heresy to the average farm labourer, a *low alcohol* cider. The opinion of the average Somerset cider drinker of TCC's best-selling blends would not normally be printable in a book of this nature. Set beside the rarer individual ciders, still, deep and misty, TCC's mass-produced brands taste distinctly uninteresting. But you could do worse than to try the local brand, Natch. TCC know how to make cider and may fairly argue that it is simply catering for national tastes. How much those tastes have been shaped by the marketing campaigns of the large companies is another matter. TCC has a visitor centre at Norton Fitzwarren which recounts the cidermaking process and invariably leads visitors to Morses Place, a cider pub run by the company. Personally, I find a visit to Sheppy's much more rewarding.

The most interesting item in Taunton is the castle, though it is almost hidden by the modern town centre. This was an ancient site for a fortification, certainly occupied as early as Saxon times. There are remains of a Norman keep in the nearby Castle Hotel while the castle itself is principally 13th century. Today it houses the county museum, the local history library and the Somerset Archeological and Natural History Society. The museum has an excellent display on the Monmouth Rebellion. The notorious Judge Jeffreys held court in the Great Hall of the castle, hanging and deporting so-called traitors on the flimsiest of evidence. The displays, from Stone Age through the Roman era to more recent times, are a far cry from the dusty image of the traditional county museum. There are a few old houses off the High Street but Taunton, while a pleasant, unhurried town, has little else to offer by comparison with the county's other sights.

East of Taunton

The commonest way out of the county from Taunton is north, to Bath and Bristol, or south to Exeter. A less frequent route is to the east, and it is an enjoyable one for the visitor who wishes to travel on into Dorset without seeing east Devon.

Once again, the Arthurian connotations are strong and have led to the legend that the fabled king's city of Camelot stood at Cadbury Castle, the fortified hill that rises above South Cadbury, five miles east of Yeovilton. The hill fort is certainly impressive even for doubters of the local tale that the king sleeps in a cave within and each Midsummer Eve rides around it with his knights. Cadbury is another of the region's early settlements based on a natural fortification. There was a Neolithic community here and later Iron Age Celts surrounded the hill with enormous banks and ditches which survive today. The inhabitants were massacred by the Romans around AD 70, presumably for some civil disobedience, since this was 26 years after the invasion and could not have been part of the military defence against Rome.

During the Dark Ages, the 'time of Arthur', it is clear that Cadbury was the capital of a powerful regional ruler, perhaps the legendary king himself. The rubble of walls from earlier ramparts was used to make new defences, and there is evidence that a large communal hall existed at the top of the hill. The Arthurian connection comes from the writing of Leland who recorded: 'At the very south ende of the chirch of South-Cadbyri standith Camallate, sumtyme a famose toun or castelle, apon a very torre or hille wunderfully enstrengthened of nature, to which be 2 enteringes up by very stepe way… In the upper part of the coppe of the hille be 4 diches or trenches, and a balky waulle of yerth betwixt every one of them… Much gold, sylver and coper of the Romaine coynes hathe be found ther yn plowing… Ther was found in hominum memoria a horse shoe of sylver at Camallate. The people can tell nothing ther but that they have hard say that Arture much resortid to Camalate.' Unfortunately, Leland was writing in the 16th century, probably a millennium after Arthur, even if he existed, died. It's a good story though.

The road east from Taunton can lead to several small, charming towns, largely off the beaten tourist track. Ilminster, to the south, is one of the most memorable, a pretty rural community largely bypassed by the roar and volume of modern traffic which has damaged some of its neighbours. This is the country of Ham stone, the golden limestone quarried from around Ham Hill near Montacute, a material which has now given its name to the local borough council (its neighbour, to the east, is known, of course, as Camelot). The marketplace of Ilminster shows Ham stone at its best. The minster, the parish church of St Mary, is an imposing pile for such a small community, dating from the 14th century. To the north is the National Trust's Barrington Court, again in Ham stone. It is a Tudor manor house built by the first Earl of Bridgewater and restored in the 1920s by the sugar magnate Colonel A. Lyle, with beautiful gardens influenced by Gertrude Jekyll. The house is leased to a furniture reproduction company, Stuart Interiors, which displays its wares there.

Ilminster should not be confused with its near namesake, Ilchester, which lies to the north east and betrays its Roman origins almost every time a local gardener digs his allotment. This was once the site of a large Roman encampment. Today there are a few Georgian houses but little more, though aviation enthusiasts will be drawn to nearby Yeovilton. This is the home of the Fleet Air Arm Museum, a positive cornucopia of aircraft historic and modern, among them the original prototype for Concorde, flown here for honourable retirement after it had completed its task.

Yeovil itself has little of interest and is merely a busy, expanding commercial town of pleasant aspect, though the church of St John, from the same mason who designed Wells cathedral, is memorable. There are two exceptional country houses nearby. Brympton d'Evercy is a privately-run estate with a lovely old house. There is an active vineyard and a still which makes the apple brandy, calvados, from local apples. Montacute House is one of the National Trust's principal glories in the region, a 16th-century mansion in landscaped grounds with a famous long gallery. There is a collection of Elizabethan and Jacobean portraits on loan from the National Portrait Gallery and fine 17th- and 18th-century furniture.

Crewkerne, south west of Yeovil, is a pretty small town of Georgian leanings off the A30 while Castle Cary, to the north, is a characterful little place with good local shops and a slightly eccentric nature. There is an 18th-century lock-up, the 'Pepper Pot', once used for housing the town drunks, and a curious town hall of 17th- and 19th-century origins. Somerton, which claims to have been the capital of ancient Wessex, is now a peaceful little market town of much charm, particularly around the old marketplace. Nearby is the National Trust's Lyte's Cary, a medieval manor house and chapel built from local Keinton stone. The property was restored in 1910 and is surrounded by a working farm.

Beyond the towns lie scores of interesting villages. East Coker, near to Yeovil, is a slumbering hamlet unmoved by the bustle of its neighbour; the poet T. S. Eliot is buried in the village churchyard. And places with evocative names – Kingsbury Episcopi, Curry Rivel, Queen Camel, Compton Paucefoot, and Marston Magna – make interesting destinations for an aimless afternoon's drive away from the tourist crowds.

At the eastern perimeter of the county lies Wincanton. On mundane days it is simply an unremarkable country town overlooking the Blackmoor Vale. On race days, when the National Hunt meetings take place, this is transformed into a picturesque community of jockeys, bookmakers and punters anxious to cast the runes for the winner of the next gallop. It is a pleasant spot to shed a few pounds and from here the A303 runs fast to the east, with excellent road connections for London, Salisbury and Marlborough to the north.

Penniless Porch and the Cathedral, Wells

Tourist Information

(* denotes a seasonal service only)

Town Hall
Market Place
Wells
Tel: 0749 72552/75987

1 Marchant's Buildings
Glastonbury*
Tel: 0458 32954

The Library
Corporation Street
Taunton
Tel: 0823 274785

Hotels

Castle Hotel
Castle Green
Taunton
Somerset
Tel: 0823 272671
Historic inn now one of the most
luxurious hotels in the region. Not for the
budget-conscious.
Rooms: 35
Credit cards: Access, Visa, Amex, Diners
Rating *****

Heatherton Grange
Bradford-on-Tone
Taunton
Somerset
Tel: 0823 461777
Countryside inn handy for Taunton.
Rooms: 17
Credit cards: Access, Visa, Amex, Diners
Rating ***

Old Manor Farmhouse
Norton Fitzwarren
Taunton

Somerset
Tel: 0823 289801
Charming farmhouse accommodation
with one-acre garden in cider country.
Rooms: 8
Credit cards: Access, Visa, Diners
Rating ***

George & Pilgrims Hotel
1 High Street
Glastonbury
Somerset
Tel: 0458 31146
Historic pilgrims' inn with characterful
four-poster bedrooms. Some
accommodation is in uninspiring modern
wing and, at the time of writing, the hotel
is undergoing a change of ownership.
Rooms: 14
Credit cards: Access, Visa, Amex, Diners
Rating ****

No3
3 Magdalene Street
Glastonbury
Somerset
Tel: 0458 32129
Acclaimed hotel and restaurant in
Georgian house next to abbey.
Rooms: 3
Credit cards: Visa, Amex
Rating *****

Ancient Gate House Hotel
Sadler Street
Wells
Somerset
Tel: 0749 72029
Old hotel convenient for the centre of
Wells, with Italian restaurant.
Rooms: 10
Credit cards: Access, Visa, Amex, Diners
Rating ***

Swan Hotel
Sadler Street
Wells

Somerset
Tel: 0749 78877
The city's foremost coaching inn, dating
from the 15th century, facing the west
front of the cathedral.
Rooms: 32
Credit cards: Access, Visa, Amex, Diners
Rating ****

Private Accommodation

Tumblers
Kilmersdon
Somerset
Tel: 0761 34452
Pretty old cottage by stream well situated
for Glastonbury or Bath.
Rooms: 2
Credit cards: none
Rating **

Whittles Farm
Beer Crocombe
8m SE Taunton
Somerset
Tel: 0823 480301
Rooms on a working 200-acre farm.
Rooms: 4
Credit cards: none
Rating **

Restaurants

No3
3 Magdalene Street
Glastonbury
Somerset
Tel: 0458 32129
Beautiful classic food with an emphasis
on West Country fish and shellfish,
lobster a speciality. Booking advisable.
Credit cards: Visa, Amex
Rating *****

George & Pilgrims Hotel
1 High Street
Glastonbury
Somerset
Tel: 0458 31146
Lovely old dining room, English cooking
with style.
Credit cards: Access, Visa, Amex, Diners
Rating ****

Castle Hotel
Castle Green
Taunton
Somerset
Tel: 0823 272671
One of the West Country's most famous
restaurants, with fine fresh gourmet food
of the highest standards. Expect to pay
for it.
Credit cards: Access, Visa, Amex, Diners
Rating *****

Rugantinos
Sadler Street
Wells
Somerset
Tel: 0749 72029
Friendly Italian restaurant attached to the
Ancient Gate House hotel – tournedos,
pasta and other Italian classics.
Credit cards: Access, Visa, Amex, Diners
Rating ***

Round Table
Crown Hotel
Glastonbury
Salmon, mussels, oysters and game
feature regularly on an ambitious menu.
Credit cards: Access, Visa
Rating ****

Historic Houses

Barrington Court (NT)
5m NE Ilminster
Model estate and farm buildings
influenced by the garden designer

Barrington Court contd
Gertrude Jekyll. March to November 11-5, closed Thursdays and Fridays.

King John's Hunting Lodge (NT)
The Square
Axbridge
Tudor merchant's house now a museum of local history and archeology. March-September 2-5 daily.

Lyte's Cary Manor (NT)
4m N Ilchester
Medieval manor house and chapel with attractive gardens. March-October Wednesdays and Saturdays 2-5.30.

Montacute House (NT)
4m W Yeovil
Imposing 16th-century mansion with fine furniture collection and portraits on loan from the National Portrait Gallery. March to October 12.30-5 closed Tuesdays.

Brympton d'Evercy
Yeovil
Picturesque country house, county life museum, gardens, vineyard and winery. Manufacturer of English apple brandy/calvados. May to September 2-6, closed Thursdays and Fridays.

Gaulden Manor
Tolland
Nr Taunton
Small manor dating from the 12th century once the home of the Turbervilles - Hardy's d'Urbervilles. Opening times vary, confirm on 09847 213.

Forde Abbey
Nr Chard
Originally a Cistercian monastery, Forde lies in a gorgeous location surrounded by 30 acres of 18th-century gardens. Gardens open daily 10-4.30, house Easter to mid October Wednesdays, Sundays and Bank Holidays 2-5.30.

Ancient Monuments

Cadbury Castle
South Cadbury
Iron Age Celtic hill fort used as Saxon defence. First said to be original site of Arthur's Camelot by a Tudor writer; the idea has stuck. Open all year.

Glastonbury Abbey
Glastonbury
Ruins of Arthurian abbey covering 36 acres. Daily 9.30-dusk.

Museums

Fleet Air Arm Museum
Royal Naval Air Station
Yeovilton
More than 50 historic aircraft including early Concorde. Daily 10-5.30 summer, 10-4.30 winter.

Glastonbury Tribunal (EH)
Glastonbury
Medieval house in the High Street once used as the abbey courthouse. Now houses the museum of Glastonbury Antiquarian Society. Open summer daily 10-6; winter daily 10-4, ex Monday.

The Shoe Museum
High Street
Street
Part of the old Clark factory in Somerset's leading shoe town. Displays of shoes from Roman times and the local industry in its heyday. Easter to October 10-4.45 Monday to Friday, 10-4.30 Saturdays.

Somerset Rural Life Museum
Abbey Farm

Chilkwell Street
Glastonbury
Lively rural museum in old farmhouse with regular displays which include cheese and buttermaking and cider crafts. March to October 10-5 weekdays, 2-6 weekends, rest of year 10-5 weekdays, 2.30-5 weekends.

Wells Museum
Cathedral Green
Wells
The remains of 'the witch of Wookey Hole', an early cave inhabitant, always attracts attention. Geology and archeology feature too, with displays about the great cathedral. Easter to September Monday to Saturday 10-5.30, Sundays 11-5.30, rest of year Wednesday to Sunday 11-4.

County Museum
The Castle
Taunton
Comprehensive regional displays, including some devoted to the Pitchfork rebellion with which the town is so bloodily associated. Judge Jeffrey's murderous assize court was held in the Castle. Monday to Saturday 10-5.

Other Diversions

Willows and Wetlands Centre
Meare Green Court
Stoke St Gregory
Taunton
Display of traditional willow craft in the wetlands, on the Curry Moor Trail. 9-1, 2-5, Monday to Saturday.

Wookey Hole Caves
Wookey Hole Mill
Wells
Spectacular caves now a sizable tourist attraction with waxworks, waterwheel

and working paper mill. 9.30-5.30 summer, 10.30-4.30 winter.

The Truckle of Cheese
33 High Street
Glastonbury
Tel: 0458 32116
Excellent cheese shop and delicatessen with local farm produce.

Falkland Islands Agency
Falkland House
Tucker Street
Wells
Tel: 0749 77902
Sweaters, jewellery, fleeces and wool imported from the Falklands.

Cricket Malherbie Farms
Stowey Court
Nether Stowey
Bridgwater
Working cheese and dairy farm. See cheddar being made, cream, butter, cider for sale. April to September 8-5.30 Monday to Saturday, Thursdays 8-8, Sundays and Bank Holiday Mondays 10-5.30. Rest of the year 8-5 Monday to Saturday.

Perry's Cider Mills
Dowlish Wake
Nr Ilminster
Traditional cider farm using local apples; collection of old wagons and displays of corn dollies. Close to Cricket Malherbie (see above). Weekdays 9-1, 1.30-5.30, Saturdays 9.30-1, 2-4.30, Sundays 9.30-1.

Taunton Cider Mill
Norton Fitzwarren
Working cider mill producing well-known brands like Dry Blackthorn. Visits are best booked on 0823 283141 (weekdays) 0823 283145 weekends. Casual visitors can join tours at 3pm every Thursday.

Sheppy's Cider Farm
Three Bridges
Bradford-on-Tone
Tel: 0823 461233
Prize-winning family cider firm in the
valley of Taunton Deane. May to
September Monday to Saturday, 8.30-7;
rest of year 8.30-6. Sundays noon-2 Easter
to Christmas only.

Gothic Image
7 High Street
Glastonbury
Occult and mystical bookshop with a vast
collection of Arthurian and other tomes.

Whatley Vineyard and Herb Garden
Frome
Vineyard and walled herb garden,
signposted from the A361. Easter to
October 10-6, closed Mondays except
Bank Holidays.

Pilton Manor Vineyard
Pilton
Well regarded vineyard with winebar
between Glastonbury and Shepton
Mallet. May to September 11-5
Wednesday to Sunday. Conducted tours
must be booked on 074 989 325.

Moorlynch Vineyard
Bridgwater
Wine bar and walks on 16-acre farm with
some rare farm animals. May to
September 10-6.

Regency Terrace, Sidmouth

6 East Devon

Exeter, the county town of Devon, is the starting point for a tour of the principal sights of the eastern end of the region. This is one of the less visited parts of a county popular with visitors for more than a century. Exeter, while a busy commercial centre, has a magnificent cathedral, a famous maritime museum and a rich collection of historic buildings. To the east, lie the unspoilt resorts of Exmouth, Budleigh Salterton and Sidmouth. Inland lie the interesting towns of Ottery St Mary, birthplace of the poet Samuel Taylor Coleridge, the lace town of Honiton, and Axminster, famous for its carpets. Hotels in Exeter cater principally for the business trade; there are more relaxed places to stay in the coastal resorts. Devon, for many visitors, is the most distant part of Wessex; weekend breaks may need to extend to three or four days. Any of the coastal towns provides a good base for visiting the area; all of the major sights are within easy reach by car.

Exeter

Devon is a large and varied county, running from the English Channel in the south to the Bristol Channel in the north. Exmoor, Dartmoor and the Torquay area are the magnets for the modern visitor, busy, well-

117

documented tourist areas that groan at the seams at the height of summer. But there is more to the county than this.

The bustle of modern commercial life envelops Exeter so much that the visitor may be tempted to give the city short shrift. This would be a mistake. After Bristol and Bath, this is the most interesting city of the West Country, and one with a rich heritage and history for the traveller willing to delve underneath the surface. Exeter can occupy an interesting day.

Exeter was the most important city of the West Country in medieval times but also had significance for the Romans. They had a fortified town here, at the end of the famous Icknield Way, the Roman road which crossed the country from east to west. The Dark Ages brought in the chaos and confusion we have seen elsewhere, but the conquering Normans, seeing the strategic importance of the site, built a new castle, Rougemont, of which traces remain. In the 11th century, the growing town became the centre of monastic power in the region and, in 1107, work began on the building which was, after many changes, to become the present cathedral.

The early wealth of Exeter was based on wool and trade. There was an active weaving community selling its wares direct to London and the Continent. The principal port for shipping these goods was the pretty little town of Topsham, now almost a suburb of the city downstream on the Exe before Exmouth, and the charges levied by the burgers of Topsham for Exeter trade were a constant source of resentment. In the mid-16th century, the city paid for a canal to be built which would enable the construction of docks in Exeter itself, thus bypassing Topsham. The work cost £5,000 and pioneered the use of sophisticated locks for raising and lowering the level of water. The canal was enlarged a century later to take larger ships and, by the beginning of the 18th century, was able to cope with vessels of 300 tons. The port of Exeter, in its prime, had 230 ships of its own trading regularly with the Continent, but the trade disappeared almost overnight with the introduction of the railways which provided a faster and more inexpensive link with the rest of the country.

The seafaring past of Exeter, active as it was, would be of little interest to the modern visitor had it not led to the creation of the city's Maritime Museum, as happy a collection of boats and nautical bric-a-brac as can be found anywhere in the country. Even if there were nothing else of interest in the city, the museum would demand the visitor's attention.

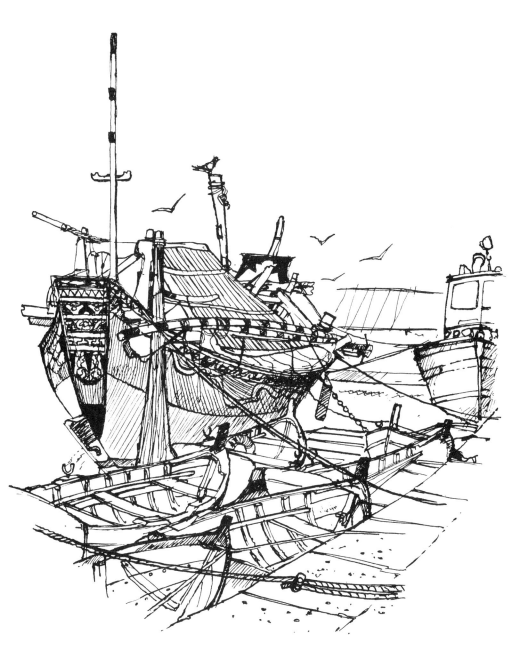

Exeter Maritime museum

It is located in the old Quay, with its medieval warehouses, a site much favoured by television and film producers looking for nautical backgrounds (much of the BBC's *Onedin Line* was filmed here). The collection of river and sea craft is catholic in the extreme, embracing Oriental junks, traditional English fishing smacks, Venetian gondolas, Welsh coracles and oddities like the obscure Yugoslav 'Chun'. Brunel's Bertha, the world's oldest working steam vessel, John Fairfax's single-handed Transatlantic rowing boat Britannia, and the Puffin, found mysteriously floating in mid-Atlantic in the 1960s without her two man crew, are among the exhibits. The museum is a serious restoration body run by the International Sailing Craft Association whose shipwrights may be found working on ancient sails or repairing rotting timberwork. Visitors are welcome to clamber on board many of the vessels and children are welcome to turn capstans or work the odd windlass. All in all, a marvellous and intelligent visitor attraction which will surely help revive Exeter's tourist fortunes. From the Quay, too, it is possible to catch pleasure boats downstream on the Exe or even out into the Channel and west to Torquay.

The centre of Exeter retains several interesting old buildings, more than it perhaps deserves. In 1942 the city was the subject of a disastrous German bombing raid which destroyed much of the old Georgian area and part of the cathedral. The city has restored what it can and redeveloped the rest.

The Gothic cathedral, with its close, is a natural magnet for the visitor. While Norman and traces of Saxon work remain, the bulk of the building was completed in the 14th century under the control of Bishop Grandisson, who was responsible for the very similar collegiate church of Ottery St Mary (see p.125). Exeter combines different variations of the architectural style known as Gothic and is of much interest to those who specialise in church architecture. The untutored visitor to Wessex will doubtless wish to compare it with the other great cathedral of the region, that of Salisbury, built around the same time but of different proportions. Exeter is low, almost squat, more the broad-beamed monk than Salisbury's elegant, ascetic scholar. Inside the cathedral tells a different tale. The vast ribbed ceiling, supported on ribbed columns, is a complex and delightful web of geometric stone, making Exeter one of those rare cathedrals which is as eye-catching inside as out. The bishop's throne – proof positive of the power held by the clergy of the time – is famous and dates from the early 14th century. There is an interesting minstrels' gallery, dating from the time when a variety of musicians accompanied the choir, and several intriguing figures on the choir screen, among them an elephant. The plethora of memorials, many to earlier bishops, is too large to document and should be treated as a register of noble deaths recorded in stone. The clock, on the north transept, dates from the 14th century and nearby can be seen a rare medieval wall painting of the Resurrection.

The Close, with its Palace and Deanery, cannot stand comparison with Salisbury. Carry on into the High Street to find the remaining buildings of medieval Exeter. The Guildhall claims to be the oldest civic building still in use in the country. Most of it was built in the late 15th century though parts could be up to 300 years older. Around Rougemont Gardens, site of the original Norman castle, can be found the museums of Rougemont House and the Royal Albert Memorial. Close by, closed at the time of writing but due to reopen, are the underground passages built to supply the medieval city with water. Though well lit, they are not suitable for those afraid of enclosed spaces. St Nicholas Priory, originally the guest wing of a Benedictine Priory, has now been restored to the condition of an Elizabethan gentleman's house, with period furniture.

Exeter, for all its attractions, is a city that is only beginning to come to terms with the needs of the modern visitor, but it is doing so with gusto. The free walking tours run by the Corps of Voluntary City Guides, details of which are available from the tourist information centre, are an excellent introduction to the city and cover some points which would be difficult for the newcomer to find, even with a detailed handbook. Occasional theme walks – the city canals and the effects of the Blitz – are also organised, and the author can only recommend them.

Exmouth

From Exeter, the visitor to east Devon crosses the Exe, either by the old main road into Dorset or the modern motorway, then heads due south along the A376, following the line of the Exe estuary. Exmouth lies at the very tip of the estuary, separated from Dawlish Warren on the western side by a narrow channel of water. There is a touch of Brighton to the town, obvious even before one learns that this is the oldest seaside resort in the county. The grand old dame of the West Sussex coast and this Devonian matron share the same antecedents: patronised by nobility in the 18th century, popularised by the common people in Victorian times,

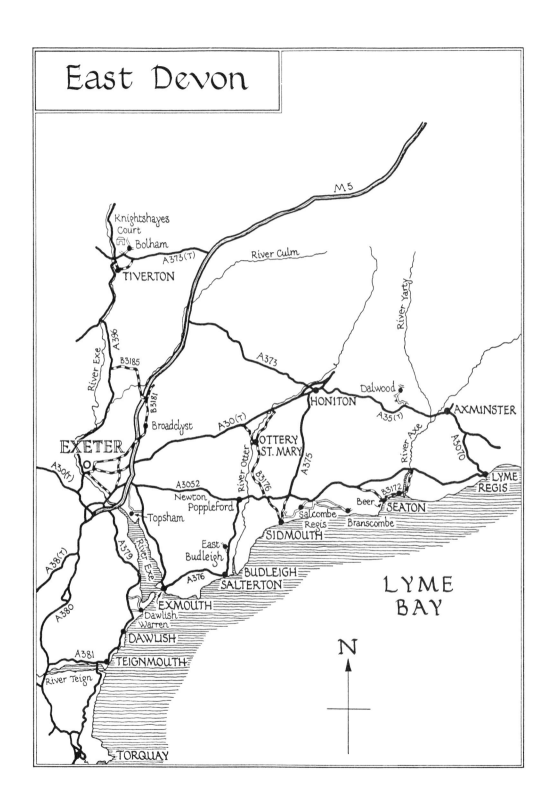

East Devon

M.5

Knightshayes
Court
Bolham
A373(T)
TIVERTON
River Culm

River Exe
A396
B3185
B3181
Broadclyst
A30(T)
River Yarty
Dalwood
HONITON
A35(T)
River Axe
AXMINSTER
A3010
EXETER
A30(T)
OTTERY
ST. MARY
River Otter
B3176
A375
A3052
LYME
REGIS
Newton
Poppleford
B3172
Beer
SEATON
Topsham
Salcombe
Regis
Branscombe
East
Budleigh
SIDMOUTH
A38(T)
A379
River Exe
A376
BUDLEIGH
SALTERTON
LYME
BAY
A380
EXMOUTH
Dawlish
Warren
DAWLISH
N
A381
TEIGNMOUTH
River Teign
TORQUAY

somewhat devastated by the death of the family British holiday trade since the 1960s. There is the same faded charm and selection of handsome, crumbling buildings, though Exmouth does not stand on the same scale as Brighton and its sister town of Hove.

There was a Roman harbour here, but the town was, for centuries, effectively little more than an extension of the port of Exeter. Exmouth sent one ship, the Felix, to join the Armada fleet, and was later involved in trade to Newfoundland and the Mediterranean based on cod fishing, a common living pursued by British seaports in the West Country and East Anglia from the 16th century onwards. Its range may come as a surprise to the modern reader. Men from Exmouth and the like would sail for Newfoundland and return, many month later, laden with salted cod. These same boats would then trade the cod for wine and other exotic goods in the Mediterranean ports of Spain and Italy, returning with their goods to England. Cadiz, Brindisi and the cold shores of Newfoundland were familiar sights to the average Exmouth sailor of the 17th century.

Now there is an active little fishing fleet which sells its catch locally, and very good it is too. There is a fine beach and walks in both directions, and local pleasure boats to Exeter and other destinations. It is not the most characterful resort of the east Devon coast – Budleigh Salterton and Sidmouth must vie for that title – but Exmouth, with all its commercialism, does not grate in the way that some of its contemporaries do.

A few curiosities deserve mention. La Ronde is a circular Georgian house open to the public and displaying a shell gallery of local finds. The design is supposedly based on an Italian basilica of the 6th century seen by two Exmouth women, Jane and Mary Parminter, while they were making the 'Grand Tour' of Europe. Many will doubtless be fascinated by 'The Wonderful World of Miniature' on the seafront which houses what it claims is the world's largest 00 gauge model railway line. The track covers more than 7,500 feet with up to 20 trains working at one time, and is open from Easter until November. There is a lifeboat exhibition and some excellent sea angling, all happily housed cheek-by-jowl with the existing commercial activities of the port. The eagle-eyed may even spot the guilty secret of the great cidermaking firms here, for a regular trade in Exmouth is the apple juice tanker, unloading thousands of gallons of compressed Golden Delicious. This tasteless stuff is the cheap raw material which keeps the big manufacturers going in place of the true cider apples which were once the sole source of the West Country's most famous drink.

Exmouth's popularity with the upper classes seems to have left it with a legacy of broken patrician hearts. Lady Nelson, deserted by her husband for Lady Hamilton, pined away here for many years and is buried in the church at nearby Littleham. Her home was at 6, The Beacon; a few doors away, at number 19, was the second wife of the wayward poet Lord Byron who led a similarly deserted life while her husband pursued his literary and romantic career elsewhere.

Budleigh Salterton

From Exmouth the road runs east, sadly behind the coast, to reach the little resort of Budleigh Salterton at the mouth of the River Otter. This is a delightful area much associated with that famous Devonian Sir Walter Raleigh who was born at East Budleigh. One of our most famous images of Raleigh, in Millais's painting of Raleigh's childhood, depicts the explorer listening to the tales of an old fisherman on Budleigh beach. Millais loved Budleigh and lived for a time on the seafront.

Raleigh was a member of a famous Devonian family and, in spite of an undeserved end at the executioner's axe, was one of the major figures of the Elizabethan age: explorer, navigator and writer. His first wife is buried in East Budleigh church where the family arms can be found on one of the carved benches.

Budleigh, for reasons it is hard to fathom, has escaped the vagaries which afflict so many small modern resorts. It is smart, pleasant and disarmingly compact, a picture of leisurely small town England, which is doubtless why that arch-satirist P. G. Wodehouse depicted his gentry retiring to the place. Fishing boats lie upturned on the beach waiting for the next foray in search of the elusive cod and plaice, substantial Georgian and Victorian villas maintain a quiet life behind the curtains of the narrow town streets, and all around is the fine coastline of east Devon, in part composed of red sandstone.

Walking is the principal leisure occupation of Budleigh, and one may well meet a few escaped characters from a Wodehouse novel in the process. There is a nice trek out to the slim mouth of the Otter to the east. Near here, probably in Roman times, were the salt beds which gave the town its name. The mouth of the Otter is so narrow that you can throw a pebble across from the western side. A local tale has it that you will return to Budleigh if the pebble sticks in the sandstone of the opposing cliff, but I suspect many will return to Budleigh regardless, for it is a relaxing, if not downright soporific, place.

Ottery St Mary

East Devon's remaining coastal resort of any size, Sidmouth, should probably be reserved for last, since the seaside towns, while charming, can become repetitive. Ottery, five miles inland, is a reminder that Devon can be just as welcoming away from the coast. With little more than 5,000 permanent residents, the place could scarcely merit the designation town were it not for the vast collegiate church, largely based on the design of Exeter cathedral.

Ottery is one of the most important parish churches of the county and dates mainly from the early 14th century. There is a medieval clock and several grand tombs from differing centuries. The weathercock on the tower is, at 500 years old, supposed to be one of the earliest still in use in Europe, a claim which seems hard to challenge. Through a peculiarity of design, it produced a drone when the wind was in the right direction and of sufficient force. Earlier this century, some bright spark took to restoring the piece and inadvertently changed the drone to an unpleasant howl, with the result that the weathercock is now firmly stoppered and silent, though it points out the wind direction admirably. The grandeur of the church, while still somewhat daunting, is not what it was. Cromwell's puritanical men stripped the building of its decorations when they failed to recruit volunteers from the town for the siege of Exeter.

One of the parish vicars, commemorated on a plaque in the church, was the Rev. John Coleridge, father of the poet Samuel Taylor Coleridge, the most famous son of Ottery and Devon's foremost literary figure. Coleridge spent his boyhood by the banks of the Otter, though he had little connection in later life when his most famous work, the *Rime of the Ancient Mariner,* was written in a haze of opium. He did, however, produce one work about his birthplace, *Sonnet to the River Otter.*

Ottery has several attractive streets, mainly Georgian, all of them now well marked out on a heritage trail through the town. The walk makes for a pleasant half day, and there are several reliable pubs in town for lunch. Three annual events deserve mention. Each Guy Fawkes' Night, the men of Ottery roll lighted tar barrels through the streets, a somewhat dangerous occupation requiring the binding of hands to avoid being burned. It is a popular event, with the right kind of audience-endangering atmosphere to be vaguely reminiscent of running the bulls in Pamplona, though rather less hazardous. On Pixie Day, a piece of pure tourist 'folklore' usually in June, the children of the town dress as pixies and scamper round the place 'arresting' pretty much whomsoever they please. Pixies, mischievous country spirits – a role for which Ottery children, like those everywhere, are well suited – are supposed to have been the original occupants of Ottery. One of the smaller delights of east Devon is that, Ottery apart, the traveller can usually avoid the proliferation of pixie paraphernalia which clogs the north of the county and overwhelms Cornwall. The tourist information office will tell you when the festival takes place each year so that you may make your own choice. Finally, Ottery stages, each July, a jazz festival which, like everything else in this ambitious little place, seems to defy the size of its surroundings.

Ottery St Mary

Sidmouth

The most easterly of the main coastal resorts, Sidmouth has all of Budleigh's charm and a fair measure of its own besides. There is a busy little fishing fleet and a shingle beach which will not appeal to the lover of Mediterranean sand. The town has prospered for nearly two centuries on its reputation as a distinguished seaside town for the journeying middle and upper classes. Royalty and large sections of Debretts have provided it with a steady income, backed by the patronage of those who always follow where the red carpets lead. Today there is a touch of the tawdry in the air, but not so much that it will spoil the stay of most visitors.

The town lies in the Sid valley between the red sandstone cliffs of the east Devon coastline, with bracing walks in both directions. Large parts of the centre of town remain Georgian and Victorian, pleasantly laid out and well maintained. The faint but discernible aroma of mothballs and the gentle drone of afternoon snoozing is apparent everywhere, but the place is none the worse for that. There is an annual folk festival during the first week of August and later in the same month a regatta week, while each June sees a local arts festival of principally domestic talent. There is little of cultural interest, though Queen Victoria, who spent several childhood holidays in the town, did donate a stained glass window to the parish church.

To the east lie two little villages of unspoilt attraction. Salcombe Regis, set inland behind Dunscombe Cliffs, is a peaceful, bucolic hamlet with an interesting church, part Norman, part Early English, and part 17th century. The village is a hearty walk from Sidmouth, either along the top of the cliffs or by the beach. Branscombe, a half hour drive to the east from Sidmouth, is a pretty thatched village which has accounted for many miles of photographic film. There are a few fishing boats which venture out from the pebble beach. Occasionally, pieces of amber have been found here, attracting precious stone hunters from miles around. Further west lies the busy little tourist village of Beer, of perennial popularity with lovers of sandy beaches. Souvenir shops now dominate the single main street, full of local lace – Beer supplied lace for the wedding dress of Queen Victoria – and less genuine ephemera. Historic Beer, a smuggling village of ruthless endeavour and a quarry town which supplied stone for Exeter and Winchester cathedrals, is somehow engulfed in this modern trade, but there is some harmless enjoyment to be had on the mackerel fishing expedition trips from the beach and rootling around the rock pools revealed by the low tide.

Budleigh Salterton

Tourist Information

(* denotes a seasonal service only)

Civic Centre
Paris Street
Exeter
Tel: 0392 265297

Exeter Services Area
Sandygate (M5)
Exeter
Tel: 0392 37581

Alexandra Terrace
Exmouth*
Tel: 0395 263744

Fore Street
Budleigh Salterton*
Tel: 03954 5275

The Old Town Hall
The Flexton
Ottery St Mary*
Tel: 04081 3964

Angel Hotel Car Park
High Street
Honiton*
Tel: 0404 3716

The Old Courthouse
Church Street
Axminster*
Tel: 0297 34386

Hotels

Salston Manor
Ottery St Mary
Devon
Tel: 040481 5581
Large country hotel with indoor pool,
squash courts, sauna and solarium.
Rooms: 27
Credit cards: Access, Visa, Amex, Diners
Rating ****

Fluxton Farm
Ottery St Mary
Devon
Tel: 04081 2818
Traditional Devon longhouse with two
acres of gardens.
Rooms: 10
Credit cards: none
Rating **

Lord Haldon Hotel
Dunchideok
Exeter
Devon
Tel: 0392 832483
Quiet country house hotel close to the
city.
Rooms: 20
Credit cards: Access, Visa
Rating ***

Imperial
The Esplanade
Exmouth
Devon
Tel: 0395 274761
Traditional smart seaside hotel now in
the hands of THF.
Rooms: 58
Credit cards: Access, Visa, Amex, Diners
Rating ****

Claremont
36 Wonford Road
Exeter
Devon
Tel: 0392 74699
Inexpensive quiet accommodation in
Georgian house close to the city centre.
Rooms: 3
Credit cards: none
Rating **

Victoria Hotel
The Esplanade
Peak Hill
Sidmouth
Devon
Tel: 0395 512651
Large seafront in substantial grounds a
short walk from the town centre.
Rooms: 61
Credit cards: Access, Visa, Amex, Diners
Rating ****

Hunters Moon Hotel
Sid Road
Sidmouth
Devon
Tel: 0395 513380
Private hotel in two acres of gardens in
countryside near the River Sid.
Rooms:17
Credit cards: Access, Visa
Rating ***

Private Accommodation

The Rock House
Dunsford
Exeter
Tel: 0647 52514
Country house with 12 acres of grounds
six miles east of Exeter.
Rooms: 3
Credit cards: none
Rating ***

Restaurants

Bystock Hotel
Bystock Terrace
Exeter
Interesting fixed price menus and wide
range of steaks in quiet square near the
centre of the city.
Credit cards: Access, Visa
Rating ***

York Tapp
Royal York and Faulkner Hotel
Esplanade
Sidmouth
Tel: 0395 513043/513184
Seafood specialities in a la carte
restaurant and superior bar food.
Credit cards: Access, Visa
Rating ***

Westcliff Hotel
Manor Road
Sidmouth
Tel: 0395 513252
Six course fixed price dinner menu in
restaurant overlooking the sea.
Credit cards: Access, Visa
Rating ***

Jolly's
The Bank
Newton Poppleford
Tel: 0395 68200
Interesting vegetarian cooking at
reasonable prices.
Credit cards: Access, Visa
Rating **

Stafford Hotel
5 Cornhill
Ottery St Mary
Tel: 040 481 2025
Restaurant, bistro and cellar bar to suit
range of pockets. Selection of dishes
from home made pizzas to seafood and
game.
Credit cards: Access, Visa
Rating ***

Historic Houses

Loughwood Meeting House
Dalwood
4m W Axminster
Nonconformist place of worship built in

1653 and hardly changed. Now in the hands of the National Trust. Open all year, free.

Killerton
Broadclyst
Exeter
Lovely National Trust 18th-century house with gardens on 7,000-acre estate. Home of the Acland family since the Civil War. Rare trees and shrubs and display of clothing from the 17th century on. Good Friday to October 31, daily except Tuesday 11-6.

La Ronde
Summer Lane
Exmouth
Eccentric circular Georgian house with shell and furniture collection. Daily 10-6, Sunday 2-7.

Knightshayes Court
Bolham
2m N Tiverton
Famous gardens with terraces and topiary, set around magnificent Victorian house. Good Friday to October 31, 11-6.

Museums

Royal Albert Memorial Museum
Queen Street
Exeter
Cultural and ethnographic collections ranging from Red Indian life to Devon pottery. Tuesday to Saturday 10-5.30.

Rougemont House Museum
Castle Street
Exeter
Regency house containing period rooms with displays of costumes and Honiton lace. Restaurant and tea room with home baking. Monday to Saturday 10-5.30.

St. Nicholas Priory
The Mint, off Fore Street
Exeter
Recreation of the home of an Elizabethan merchant in the former guest wing of a Benedictine priory founded in 1070. Norman undercroft, Elizabethan kitchen and 15th-century guest hall. Tuesday to Saturday 10-1 and 2-5.30.

Exeter Guildhall
High Street
Exeter
Superb medieval guildhall still used for municipal functions. Display of civic silver. Monday to Saturday 10-5.30 unless civic functions are taking place.

Quay House Interpretation Centre
The Quay
Exeter
Audio-visual display documenting the history of the city. Daily 10-5, 10-6 July and August.

131

Index